of related interest

The Survival Guide for Newly Qualified Social Workers in Adult and Mental Health Services
Hitting the Ground Running
Diane Galpin, Jenny Bigmore and Jo Parker
ISBN 978 1 84905 158 3

The Survival Guide for Newly Qualified Child and Family Social Workers
Hitting the Ground Running
Helen Donnellan and Gordon Jack
ISBN 978 1 84310 989 1

Social Work Theories in Action
Edited by Mary Nash, Robyn Munford and Kieran O'Donoghue
Foreword by Jim Ife
ISBN 978 1 84310 249 6

The Post-Qualifying Handbook for Social Workers
Edited by Wade Tovey
ISBN 978 1 84310 428 5

Handbook for Practice Learning in Social Work and Social Care
Knowledge and Theory
2nd edition
Edited by Joyce Lishman
ISBN 978 1 84310 186 4

Social Work Education and Training
Edited by Joyce Lishman
ISBN 978 1 84905 076 0
Research Highlights in Social Work Series

Social Work with Children and Families
Getting into Practice
3rd edition
Ian Butler and Caroline Hickman
ISBN 978 1 84310 598 5

Child Protection Systems in the United Kingdom
A Comparative Analysis
Anne Stafford, Nigel Parton, Sharon Vincent and Connie Smith
ISBN 978 1 84905 067 8

Core Social Work

International Theory, Values and Practice

Willem Blok

Foreword by Stephen A. Webb

Jessica Kingsley *Publishers*
London and Philadelphia

Figures 3.24 and 3.25 from Donkers 2010 on p.116 and p.118 are reproduced by permission of
Gerard Donkers
Figure 5.1 from Herrmann and Maesen 2008 on p.134 is reproduced by permission of the
European Foundation of Social Quality

First published in 2009 in Dutch
by ThiemeMeulenhoff, The Netherlands, as *Inleiding Social Work vanuit internationaal perspectief*

This revised English edition published in 2012
by Jessica Kingsley Publishers
116 Pentonville Road
London N1 9JB, UK
and
400 Market Street, Suite 400
Philadelphia, PA 19106, USA

www.jkp.com

Library of Congress Cataloging in Publication Data
Blok, Willem, 1950-
  [Inleiding social work. English]
  Core social work : international theory, values and practice / Willem Blok ;
foreword by Stephen Webb.
      p. cm.
  "First published in 2009 in Dutch by ThiemeMeulenhoff, The Netherlands, as
Inleiding internationaal Work : vanuit internationaal perspectief."
  Includes bibliographical references and index.
  ISBN 978-1-84905-176-7 (alk. paper)
  1. Social service. I. Title.
  HV40.B544613 2012
  361.3--dc23
                        2011035733

British Library Cataloguing in Publication Data
A CIP catalogue record for this book is available from the British Library

ISBN 978 1 84905 176 7
eISBN 978 0 85700 401 7

Printed and bound in Great Britain

Dedicated to my wife Marja, love and light
in my life; and to my brother Rinus,
because of his sense of justness
and his eye for little things

Contents

Figures and drawings

Foreword

Social work is constantly required to confront new challenges from changing policy agendas, transitions in welfare delivery, the shift of focus towards service-user involvement, the rise of evidence-based practice, the challenge of globalization and neoliberal economics, and the 'professionalization' of front-line practice. These all impact directly on the delivery of services and interventions. It confronts these challenges whilst retaining a core set of values focusing on social justice, anti-oppressive practice, and the ethics of recognition. One of the distinctive features of social work is its continuing adherence to a set of progressive ethical values.

Social work research and practice have changed enormously over the last 40 years or so, with the language, knowledge-base and methods constantly evolving. While this emerging diversity of practice approaches appears quite striking, there continues to be something of a 'mainstream' even though it is navigated by fewer than before. However difficult it is to reach agreement about the exact nature and role of social work in modern societies, this mainstream is best conveyed in practice-based textbooks and student practitioner guides. Nevertheless, the architecture of any social work text is always meritorious when strongly girded by current research.

This important book by Willem Blok brings a fresh but closely considered perspective to important aspects of social work practice. In many respects, it represents a systematic treatment of the various components that make up the field of social work practice. In doing so, it lays out in a reader-friendly way the different processes and attributes that make up the complex world of social work. As a textbook that is informed by current evidence and contemporary research it is praiseworthy. The book really does show how organizing is the art of tolerating and forging relationships with this hybrid range of mediators called social workers. Guiding such a readership through the noise, ambiguities, tensions and complexities of practice is no mean feat, especially when done in such a vividly engaging and thorough manner.

Indeed, the merits of this book are precisely to be found in its versatility, in the scope and range of material traversed. In many ways it really does feel like a labour of love.

It is fair to say that this book bears the fruit of many years of research and practice experience, much of which the author gleaned through international perspectives and travels. As I have shared some of these with the author, I know that many a merry song, but not 'a song and dance', have been vocalized along the way. The book thus offers a broad horizon and one that particularly draws on and benefits from European traditions in social work. It is this ability to reach a wide audience that will help sustain the book's import and shelf life. This, the first of Willem's single-authored books in the English language, amply demonstrates the virtue of taking a well-seasoned approach to thinking about the vexed problems and contradictions faced by social work practitioners. Unlike some theorists in social work, infatuated by fashionable 'post' this that and the other, Willem Blok is not worried about issuing a straightforward statement on what he conceives to be the nature of social work. That's a technique, of course.

I know it has long been a deeply held ambition of Willem's to make this sort of systematic contribution to social work. The book demonstrates the insatiable curiosity the author has for modern social work, that verges on an encyclopaedic knowledge. It conveys an unflagging passion and commitment to the field of practice. The longstanding experience of the author across a variety of practice settings helps him marshall a range of understandings that are inevitably sourced by a deeply grounded set of ethical concerns. The value of social work is always permeating just beneath the surface of this text. Over the decades the author has shown consistent support for the oppressed, the disadvantaged and exploited; those on the receiving end of social work interventions. An investment in social justice and human transformation sits at the heart of Willem Blok's new book.

This book is a welcome contribution and will be a most useful guide for students of social work and its practitioners. I would like to hope that student and practitioners of social work invest time in reading it carefully from cover to cover.

Stephen A. Webb
Professor of Human Sciences
University of Newcastle, Australia

Preface and Acknowledgements

As in all other professions, social work is being affected by the ongoing process of globalization, in the form of vanishing borders, shrinking distances, rapid communication, waves of global migration, supranational policy, and international money streams.

Although many practitioners and teachers in the field of social work still consider their profession as related to culture and bound to language, there is a growing awareness that it is part of an international profession that is being confronted with comparable developments, that is seeking the same type of solutions, that is using familiar interventions, and that is fulfilling similar tasks in society.

The realization of this book was as international as its content. It was largely made possible by the internet, one of the main engines driving the current stage of globalization around the world. Based on many years of lecturing, research and development, especially in and for Poland, the book was written in the Netherlands, the text was edited in Canada, the Foreword was provided by a colleague in Australia, the drawings are 'made in Holland', and the book was published by Jessica Kingsley Publishers – a company with offices in London and Philadelphia for an international readership.

I am very grateful for the editing completed by Lesley Huygen and Rob Cleveland (Edmonton, Canada); they did a fine job and supported me all the way.

I would also like to thank Stephen Webb (Newcastle, Australia) for his encouragement and the Foreword.

During the lonesome process of writing, I felt supported by those who showed close interest in the progress of the work. Thank you for that.

I appreciated the friendly and helpful contacts with Stephen Jones and Caroline Walton of Jessica Kingsley Publishers (London, UK).

I would like to thank Henny Feijer (Leeuwarden, the Netherlands) and Adrian Liske (Poznan, Poland). Henny made the full-page drawings in the book; she is great at creating expressive cartoon-style images.

Adrian always supported me in good and bad times. He modernized my website, and included a special section dedicated to this book.

I hope this book will contribute to the education of social welfare professionals, as well as to a better understanding of the value of social work for a humane and democratic functioning of society.

I welcome comments and suggestions from readers.

Willem Blok
Senior Lecturer, NHL University of Applied Sciences
Leeuwarden, The Netherlands
Website: www.blok.to
E-mail: socialwork@blok.to

Introduction

Toward the end of the 19th century, it finally became possible to orient one's career in the direction of assisting people and to attend school to learn how to do it.

Modern, professional social work originated almost simultaneously in the United States of America and in Western Europe, as the first schools of Social Work were established in New York in 1898 and in Amsterdam the following year.

As the name suggests, 'social work' is concerned with both social developments and social relations within society. This was so at the beginning, it is certainly the case today, and it will probably always be true.

During the industrial revolution and the formation of democratically ruled nations in the 19th century and the first half of the 20th century, the term 'social' had negative connotations attached to it for society's elites: it was a word associated with lower class movements, labour unionism, revolution, strikes, and socialism.

In the Netherlands, following the Great Railway Strike of 1903, the number of students at the 'Educational Institution for Social Work' in Amsterdam decreased. In an effort to stem the tide, the name of the school was changed to 'School for Social Work' (in Dutch: 'School voor maatschappelijk werk'). This was done because 'social' was too easily associated with the dreaded 'socialism'. But that was not the only perceived danger. 'Besides the fear of political revolution, one was afraid the school might drive the female students "into the arms of ultra-feminism"' (van Gent 1991, p.44, translation WB).

Social work has always had two 'faces', and continues to do so: on the one hand helping people, and on the other hand supporting the established order and relations in society, even when they are controversial. In other words, the social worker is a stalwart support to needy and vulnerable citizens, and in so doing contributes to the (further) adaptation and integration of these people into the established societal order and social relations.

On a more abstract theoretical level, in the introduction to their four-volume set entitled *International Social Work*, editors Gray and Webb (2010) call these two faces 'the logic of regulation' and 'the logic of security'. 'Regulation' represents society with its institutions and rules; 'security' stands for the individual's or community's well-being, free of fear, harm, apprehension, or doubt. The authors conclude that 'the essential rationality of modern social work is ambivalently configured through these twin logics of regulation and security, which work in and through each other' (pp.xxix–xxxi).

To some extent, the dual nature of social work forms a dilemma for the social worker, depending on the society in which he or she operates. It makes a substantial difference if one social worker is operating in a country with a democratic order, respecting human rights and the freedoms of speech and association, while another works in a country where these attributes of civilization are missing or neglected.

To practise professional social work, one needs long-term education of a median or higher level in order to acquire the necessary theoretical and methodological knowledge; to develop and maintain the necessary skill sets; to gain practical experience; and to form one's own professional attitude and worldview. Essential to the final point is a sense of proportion, the capacity to empathize, the ability to put situations into proper (or different) perspective(s), and critical self-reflection.

By *self-reflection*, I mean the capacity to look at one's personal, professional, and cultural values and beliefs at a distance. Different approaches or vantage points can be very helpful to the social worker. For example, looking from a historical point of view (how was it in the past?) or by looking from a different country or culture than your own (how is it somewhere else?). Both approaches can have a strong and valuable influence on young people, including new generations of social workers, social policy makers, and managers of social institutions.

I.1 Approach

In this book, social work is described from a wide, societal perspective. This is easier in a world where the distance between people, places, and cultures is continuously diminishing as a direct result of the ongoing improvement and increasing accessibility of communication and transportation. Like many of the professions, social work is now practised in numerous countries all over the world.

Through ever-increasing waves of globalization, social workers connect and interact more often and with greater ease, and this process is resulting in a slowly but surely developing singular international identity, and a growing joint body of knowledge for social work.

The development is not new. It has been there from the beginning of the development of social work as a profession. However, the social work profession is now stronger and more widespread than ever before. Though social work is practised worldwide, there remains an unmistakable Anglo-Saxon influence over its theories and methods: it speaks volumes that terms such as 'social case work', 'multi-family work', 'outreach work', and 'empowerment' are still used in non-English professional literature and non-English vocabularies.

First and foremost, this book is meant for students of social work and related studies, for social workers, and for other professionals who are cooperating or associated with social work. It offers a view into the 'kitchen of social work' without having to open all of the cupboards.

Instead of organizational details that vary from country to country, I describe on a more general level how social work fits within a greater societal network, and what functions it fulfils.

The book is a result of many years of social work education, research, and development and is supported by the author's personal experiences in the Netherlands, in Poland, and elsewhere in the world. It aims to reflect 'the state of social work' from an international perspective.

The term 'social work' is used in this book to be consistent with the international definition of social work which will be described in the first chapter. Social work is the umbrella term for a variety of interrelated social professions in various sectors of society.

In most countries the English phrase 'social work' is translated word-for-word into their indigenous language by separately translating the adjective 'social' and the noun 'work' and joining the two into a single name. Thus, it is translated as 'Sozial Arbeit' in German, 'Travaille Social' in French, 'Trabajo Social' in Spanish, and 'Praca Socjalna' in Polish.

By far the majority of professional social workers work within and from the social infrastructure of their country. They might be employed by educational, medical, social, or administrative organizations delivering services and provisions for citizens. This social infrastructure incorporating social work is usually financed by national government from tax revenues or state-sanctioned insurance premiums. The majority of social workers are civil servants or employees of nonprofit or not-for-profit institutions.

Only a small proportion of social workers have their own business or are employed by a commercial company.

This suggests that the profession's development, the extent and character of it, as well as its facilitation and distribution over various sectors and in relation to different client groups, falls within the national government's responsibility. It is a matter of public policy based on societal values and standards, and incorporated in and ruled by (national) laws and regulations. In the future, one can expect more influence on social policy from supra-national bodies like the European Union and, therefore, on social work.

Since the position and operating space of professional social work is a political matter, it is important to promote the profession in such a way as to keep the public informed about its role and to elicit public support for its plans and ideas.

I.2 Structure

Chapter 1 is the stepping stone for the rest of the book. Based on core documents of the two most important international professional organizations – the International Federation of Social Workers (IFSW) and the International Association of Schools of Social Work (IASSW) – I describe the aim of social work and its practical application, the profession's values and standards, training and education, and the most common and well-known elements of the professional body of knowledge. Chapter 1 offers a reflection on the current state of the profession as it sets a course for further development and renewal.

In Chapters 2, 3, and 4, these professional attributes are expanded upon. I refer to commonly used theories and approaches that are directly related to the international definition of social work. It is inevitable that I make some choices and interpretations when going into detail. I discuss the topics of surviving and human needs (Chapter 2), development and change (Chapter 3), and help and support (Chapter 4) as they are connected to mainstream social work.

In Chapter 5 I make use of concepts and models from two other disciplines – public administration and political science – to analyse and clarify the position and functions of social work in society. Because social work is part of the social infrastructure, it is an important instrument of social policy. The profession is of crucial interest for the democratic functioning of society as it stimulates and supports citizen participation in many fields and at all levels of society.

Chapter 6 contains a critical description and analysis of current developments in social work, and an exploration of possible ways out and forward. The ongoing globalization process presents new conditions, problems, and opportunities. International exchange and cooperation is needed to cope with these changes in a constructive and effective way. It concerns all relevant actors: workers, teachers, managers, researchers, policy makers, and customer organizations involved in social work and social policy.

I.3 Character

This book is in the first place intended to be a textbook or a useful reference for practitioners, not as a contribution to the scientific debate in social work. It is focused on (global) similarities in social work, not on (local) differences, and so as a consequence it is oriented on the current state of actual social work – not on the latest theoretical and methodical views – as it remains unclear how these vast and varied viewpoints will affect social work's body of knowledge.

This is not to suggest that I avoid discussion or that I should hesitate to express my opinions in this book. In Chapter 3, when discussing the holistic approach in social work, I provide my own views on the development of new integrative approaches in social work; and in Chapter 6, I provide my assessment of the effects of globalization on social policy and the position of social workers – especially in Western countries, where I see the impact of market mechanisms on social institutions as limiting and threatening the effective assistance of social, (para)medical, and educational workers.

1.

Social Work

Modern, professional social work has existed for more than a century, and is practised in many countries all over the world.

There is a growing consensus among the workers, teachers, researchers, and policy makers comprising the International Federation of Social Workers (IFSW) and the International Association of Schools of Social Work (IASSW) on the aim, content, standards, and values of the social work profession, as well as in relation to its education and body of knowledge.

The joint global view on social work provided by IFSW and IASSW reflects the state of the profession, and will continue to influence the future development of it.

In this chapter I describe and explain the worldwide shared view of social work, based on major international core documents from the period 2000–2010 in which this view was established.

Close attention is paid to the aim and content of social work (Section 1.1), professional ethics (Section 1.2), social work education (Section 1.3), and the body of knowledge (Section 1.4).

Because this chapter functions as the foundation for the rest of the book, I will stay close to the original text of the core documents of IFSW and IASSW.

1.1 Aim and content

Since 1982, the IFSW has promoted and worked with a definition of social work. The latest definition as of 2000 is also supported by the IASSW. The profession of social worker is defined as follows:

> The social work profession promotes social change, problem solving in human relationships and the empowerment and liberation of people to enhance well-being.
>
> Utilizing theories of human behaviour and social systems, social work intervenes at the points where people interact with

their environments. Principles of human rights and social justice are fundamental to social work. (IFSW 2000, p. 1)

This definition provides a brief, general description of the social work profession. It answers the questions about what, how and why:

- *What?* Social workers enhance well-being in society by promoting social change, problem solving, empowerment, and liberation.

- *How?* They address the multiple, complex transactions between people and their environments through social interventions. These are goal-oriented efforts to influence the behaviour of people, groups, and organizations. These social interventions take various forms and are based on scientific theories of human behaviour and how institutions function (refer to Chapter 3).

- *Why?* The mission of social workers is 'to enable all people to develop their full potential, enrich their lives, and prevent dysfunction' (IFSW 2000, p. 1). This mission was clearly derived from the fundamental principles of human rights and social justice.

According to the IFSW (2000), social work is an interrelated system of values, theory, and practice that enables people to enhance their well-being and that of the social environment in which they live: 'As such, social workers are change agents in society and in the lives of the individuals, families and communities they serve' (p. 1).

'Development' and 'change' are inextricably bound up with life. When development stagnates, or when change is hard to achieve, people find themselves in a difficult or problematic situation. In such instances, the support of a social worker can make the difference. This is why knowledge of development and change processes, as well as the ability and skills to stimulate and support them, are an important part of the social worker's expertise. This is explored further in Chapter 3.

The support and assistance of social work is both object-oriented (problem solving and providing means for the realization of it) and subject-oriented (empowering clients to act). The social worker must also target actors who might be influencing the client insofar as they are part of the problem and/or the solution. To realize this, the social worker must be able to operate on varied levels with a variety of people (Chapter 2), fulfilling different tasks, and playing different roles dependent upon the situation (Chapter 4).

Social workers are confronted directly with the consequences of the way people interact as well as with the underlying values and standards of the involved individuals. This means that the professional expertise is of a mixed nature: instrumental (methods and techniques) on the one hand, and normative (interpretation, objectives, approach) on the other. Therefore, in all situations, with all sorts of people, the social worker must be aware of differing values and standards; be able to analyse the persons, groups, and organizations involved; and choose and implement an appropriate and effective way of working toward a solution.

The normative nature has always been characteristic of social work. As the IFSW explains:

> Social work grew out of humanitarian and democratic ideals, and its values are based on respect for the equality, worth, and dignity of all people. Since its beginnings over a century ago, social work practice has focused on meeting human needs and developing human potential. Human rights and social justice serve as the motivation and justification for social work action. In solidarity with those who are disadvantaged, the profession strives to alleviate poverty and to liberate vulnerable and oppressed people in order to promote social inclusion. (IFSW 2000, p.1)

In this respect, 'social work addresses the barriers, inequities and injustices that exist in society. It responds to crises and emergencies as well as to everyday personal and social problems' (IFSW 2000, p.1).

1.2 Professional ethics

Due to the normative character of the profession, as explained in the previous paragraph, social work requires not only the ability but also the commitment to act ethically as essential qualities offered to those who use social work services. In many countries there are (national) professional codes for social workers. These codes contain shared values and standards, serving as a guideline for the professional conduct of the social worker.

Since 1994, there has been an international professional code with principles and standards for all social workers and the institutions in which they are employed (IFSW 1994). Ten years later, this document was updated with a revised Statement of Principles, based on the international definition of social work as starting point (IFSW and IASSW 2004a).

The joint IASSW and IFSW Statement aims 'to encourage social workers across the world to reflect on the challenges and dilemmas that face them and make ethically informed decisions about how to act in each particular case (IFSW and IASSW 2004a)' Some of these problem areas include (IFSW and IASSW 2004a, p.1):

- the fact that the loyalty of social workers is often in the middle of conflicting interests

- the fact that social workers function as both helpers and controllers

- the conflicts between the duty of social workers to protect the interests of the people with whom they work and societal demands for efficiency and utility

- the fact that resources in society are limited.

The Statement of Principles refers to seven well-known, internationally accepted and recognized human rights Declarations and Conventions. These are:

- The Universal Declaration of Human Rights

- The International Covenant on Civil and Political Rights

- The International Covenant on Economic Social and Cultural Rights

- The Convention on the Elimination of all Forms of Racial Discrimination

- The Convention on the Elimination of All Forms of Discrimination against Women

- The Convention on the Rights of the Child

- Indigenous and Tribal Peoples Convention (ILO Convention 169).

These international documents are particularly relevant to social work practice and action. They function as a legitimate framework for social workers.

Two principles are elaborated upon in the international definition of social work: human rights and social justice.

The paragraph on *human rights* begins with the statement that 'social work is based on respect for the inherent worth and dignity of all people, and the rights that follow from this,' meaning that social workers 'should uphold and defend each person's physical, psychological, emotional and spiritual integrity and well-being' (IFSW and IASSW 2004a, p.2).

Therefore, social workers are called to adhere to the following (p.2):

1. Respecting the right to self-determination – Social workers should respect and promote people's right to make their own choices and decisions, irrespective of their values and life choices, provided this does not threaten the rights and legitimate interests of others.

2. Promoting the right to participation – Social workers should promote the full involvement and participation of people using their services in ways that enable them to be empowered in all aspects of decisions and actions affecting their lives.

3. Treating each person as a whole – Social workers should be concerned with the whole person, within the family, community, societal and natural environments, and should seek to recognise all aspects of a person's life.

4. Identifying and developing strengths – Social workers should focus on the strengths of all individuals, groups and communities and thus promote their empowerment.

The responsibility to stimulate social justice in society as well as in relation to the people with whom they work, means that social workers focus on (pp.2–3):

1. Challenging negative discrimination – Social workers have a responsibility to challenge negative discrimination on the basis of characteristics such as ability, age, culture, gender or sex, marital status, socio-economic status, political opinions, skin colour, racial or other physical characteristics, sexual orientation, or spiritual beliefs.

2. Recognise diversity – Social workers should recognize and respect the ethnic and cultural diversity of the societies in which they practice, taking account of individual, family, group and community differences.

3. Distributing resources equitably – Social workers should ensure that resources at their disposal are distributed fairly, according to need.

4. Challenging unjust policies and practices – Social workers have a duty to bring to the attention of their employers, policy makers, politicians and the general public situations where resources are inadequate or where distribution of resources, policies and practices are oppressive, unfair or harmful.

5. Working in solidarity – Social workers have an obligation to challenge social conditions that contribute to social exclusion, stigmatisation or subjugation, and to work towards an inclusive society.

Observing human rights and stimulating social justice directly affects social relations and the established regime in an organization, community, or country. This is much easier to accomplish in a social environment or a society that accommodates the discipline by offering space and facilities for social work. In this respect, there are noticeable differences between countries based upon living standards, culture, levels of education, ideology, religion, and the democratic nature of both local and national administrations.

In countries with an autocratic regime, where certain groups are favoured above others, and where criticism and opposition are not permitted, social workers have little or no space to effectively do their work.

It seems obvious that social work will prosper in countries with democratic constitutions that guarantee freedom of speech and association, public debate, secret ballots during an election, and minority rights. Thus, 'democracy is the belief in freedom and equality between people, or a system of government based on this belief, in which power is either held by elected representatives or directly by the people themselves' (Cambridge Dictionaries Online 2011).

It is rather ironic that in countries where social work is deeply needed, the social and political conditions for this necessary profession either do not exist or are constrained to the point of ineffectiveness.

In this respect, IFSW and IASSW should stimulate and support international surveys into the relation between the democratic nature of a community (or country) and the extent and quality of the social provisions, social benefits, social institutions, and the number of social workers being part of it. The outcome can play a role in the policy of international bodies such as the UN, the EU, the World Bank, and the IMF toward individual countries.

The final portion of *Ethics in Social Work, Statement of Principles* contains 12 general guidelines on professional conduct (IFSW and IASSW 2004a, pp.3–4). These guidelines are as follows:

1. Social workers are expected to develop and maintain the required skills and competence to do their job.

2. Social workers should not allow their skills to be used for inhumane purposes, such as torture or terrorism.

3. Social workers should act with integrity. This includes not abusing the relationship of trust with the people using their services, recognizing the boundaries between personal and professional life, and not abusing their position for personal benefit or gain.

4. Social workers should act in relation to the people using their services with compassion, empathy and care.

5. Social workers should not subordinate the needs or interests of people who use their services to their own needs or interests.

6. Social workers have a duty to take [the] necessary steps to care for themselves professionally and personally in the workplace and in society, in order to ensure that they are able to provide appropriate services.

7. Social workers should maintain confidentiality regarding information about people who use their services. Exceptions to this may only be justified on the basis of a greater ethical requirement (such as the preservation of life).

8. Social workers need to acknowledge that they are accountable for their actions to the users of their services, the people they work with, their colleagues, their employers, the professional association and to the law, and that these accountabilities may conflict.

9. Social workers should be willing to collaborate with the schools of social work in order to support social work students to get practical training of good quality and up to date practical knowledge.

10. Social workers should foster and engage in ethical debate with their colleagues and employers and take responsibility for making ethically informed decisions.

11. Social workers should be prepared to state the reasons for their decisions based on ethical considerations, and be accountable for their choices and actions.

12. Social workers should work to create conditions in employing agencies and in their countries where the principles of this statement and those of their own national code (if applicable) are discussed, evaluated and upheld.

The Statement of Principles is considered to provide a common ethical framework for social work. Conversely, national codes are more particular: 'Social workers should act in accordance with the ethical code or guidelines current in their country. These will generally include more detailed guidance in ethical practice specific to the national context' (p. 3).

1.3 Social work education

As mentioned in the Introduction, one needs to perform social work in a proper and effective way, one needs a long-term education of a median or higher level in order to acquire theoretical and methodoligical knowledge; to develop and maintain the necessary skill sets; to gain practical experience; and to form one's own professional attitude and worldview. Schools and studies of social work are nationally organized and educational endeavours can vary from a two-year diploma programme at a further education or community college to a Bachelors or Masters degree which will require three to four or five years, respectively, of intense study at university. In countries including the United States, the United Kingdom, Canada, and Australia, social work study is positioned within universities (mostly in 'Schools of Social Work').

In countries with a dualistic system of higher education, with universities on the one hand and institutions of higher applied sciences on the other, most social workers are educated in the latter. This distinction has positive and negative consequences. In universities, more emphasis is placed on theory and research in the academic tradition, while in colleges or universities of applied sciences which exist elsewhere in Europe, the focus is on arts, methods, and practice.

From an international perspective, IFSW and IASSW promote clear, joint standards for social work education. In *Global Standards for the Education and Training of the Social Work Profession* (IFSW and IASSW 2004b) these organizations established nine standards based upon the international definition of social work and on 13 core purposes of social work. I discuss the core purposes in Chapter 4, Section 1. Here my particular focus is on the educational standards.

The Global Standards focus upon the following issues:

1. The core purpose and mission of the school

2. Programme objectives and outcomes

3. Programme curricula, including field education

4. Core curricula

5. Professional staff

6. Social work students

7. Structure, administration, governance and resources

8. Cultural and ethnic diversity, and gender inclusiveness

9. Values and ethical codes of conduct.

These Global Standards establish values and principles meant to stimulate the quality of social work education and the dialogue about it. Or, in other words: 'The document reflects global standards that schools of social work should consistently aspire towards, which (collectively, and if met) would actually provide for quite sophisticated levels of social work education and training' (IFSW and IASSW 2004b, p.17).

The differences in development stages of social work between various countries are taken into account:

> The extent to which schools of social work meet the global standards will depend on the developmental needs of any given country/region and the developmental status of the profession in any given context, as determined by unique historical, socio-political, economic and cultural contexts. (IFSW and IASSW 2004b, p.17).

As examples, I examine the situation in the field of social work education in the Netherlands, Canada, Ireland, and Poland.

The Netherlands is a small European country with a well-developed system of social work and a long tradition in educating social workers that dates back to 1899 when the first school of social work was established in Amsterdam.

Today, social work in the Netherlands is practised on four levels, namely (NIZW Beroepsontwikkeling 2006):

A. Assistant

B. Practising

C. Design and implementation

D. Direction and implementation.

While two years of tertiary education is necessary for assistant positions (A) in social work, diplomas of three and four year studies at a tertiary level provide entrance to lower positions in practice (B). For design and implementation (C) a Bachelors degree (four years of study) is necessary. For direction and implementation (D), a Bachelors or Masters degree is required.

In the four-year bachelor education for social work, aspiring social workers qualify themselves in six clusters of competencies. These are:

1. Orienting, analysing, defining

2. Methodological, change-oriented social interventions

3. Working in a company or organization

4. The person of the professional worker as instrument

5. Developing research

6. Learning processes.

Another example is that of Canada. In this country, a two-year Diploma for Social Service Workers at the college level or a four-year Bachelors Degree of Social Work at the university level is required to become a social worker. Following another year of intense study in a university setting, a student can obtain a Masters Degree of Social Work.

In the Republic of Ireland social workers undertake either a four-year bachelors degree which is offered at two universities or they can qualify through postgraduate awards following an appropriate undergraduate degree in Social Studies or Social Sciences. In Ireland 'social work', which operates in a legally defined setting of duties and responsibilities, is distinguished from social care work, which traditionally has been undertaken by practitioners who may or may not be formally educated. However, social care work is now regulated and requires an Ordinary Degree in Social Studies or Social Care (Level 7) for professional registration. This takes three years to complete.

In Poland, one of the Eastern European countries with a communist past, social workers are educated at schools of social work offering a two-and-a-half-year diploma. After the fall of Communism in 1989, it became possible to study social work at universities offering three-year bachelor studies in either their sociology or pedagogy departments.

For the education of social workers, the IFSW and IASSW function in a supportive and facilitative role in the local implementation of the aforementioned global standards. To realize this, there is a need for clear mechanisms of communication across national and/or regional social work educators' associations and IASSW. Such communication could be facilitated by developing a data bank containing the details and programmes of member schools, and of national and/or regional standards and systems of quality assurance and accreditation. Such information may be shared on an international level upon request and/or via the websites of IFSW and IASSW. It is hoped that this information sharing would provide the impetus for schools of social work to aspire toward the global standards of professional social work education and training (IFSW and IASSW 2004b, pp.17–18).

With the acceptance of global standards for the education and training of social workers, the profession made an important step forward in its professionalization and profiling process. This has had, and will continue to have, positive effects on the position of social workers and the quality of their services.

1.4 Body of knowledge

During the 20th century, professional social work began collecting and distributing its expertise. Because of the specific, applied nature of the profession as well as a reliance upon theories and methods mainly developed in the USA and UK, researchers and workers often draw (and drew) from the same sources.

The dominant position of these two countries in social work is a direct result of the prevalence of the English language. More specifically, the USA has maintained its hegemony within the social work profession due to its reputation as a positive destination for immigration, which has created a large and differentiated international network of personal, professional, and business contacts.

Mel Gray and Stephen Webb (2009, 2010), who have taken up the role of 'bibliographers of social work', collected, ordered, and selected theories and methods that have continuously had an impact on thinking and operating within social work. This was a huge undertaking, considering the long history of (professional) social work. In 2009, they published an overview of 'the key ideas of authors who have contributed significantly to theoretical discussions shaping social work in recent years' (2009, p.8). In 2010, they followed with their new masterpiece

International Social Work. According to Gray and Webb, this four-volume set is meant 'to represent the diversity of viewpoints that exist in social work' and is offered as 'a major reference in social work' to researchers, students, practitioners, and policy makers (2010, p.xxvi).

The goal of these theoretical works is, however, not comparable to the goal of the book you are reading now. Here I focus on the current state of social work as it is reflected in the international definition of social work. I limit myself to well-known approaches and theories that are directly connected with, or are illustrative of, the subjects and concepts related to the international definition. This is a different, more practical approach that aligns with the educational purposes of my work: writing a study book and introduction for professionals.

According to the international definition document (IFSW 2000, p.1), social work bases its methodology 'on a systematic body of evidence-based knowledge derived from research and practice evaluation, including local and indigenous knowledge specific to its context.' The interaction between person and social environment is crucial for social work: 'it recognizes the complexity of interactions between human beings and their environment, and the capacity of people both to be affected by and to alter the multiple influences upon them including bio-psychosocial factors' (p.1). It is obvious that social work 'draws on theories of human development and behaviour and social systems to analyze complex situations and to facilitate individual, organizational, social and cultural changes' (p.1).

There is not always complete synthesis between knowledge obtained through professional practice and that discovered through scientific research. One reason for the practice-research gap is that practitioners deal with situations that are unique and idiosyncratic, while research deals with regularities and aggregates. The translation between the two is often imperfect. A hopeful development for bridging this gap is the compilation in many practice fields of collections of "best practices", largely taken from research findings, but also distilled from the experience of respected practitioners (Wikipedia 2012, p.1).

Additionally, I would like to note that the disparity between professional practice and scientific theory is bridged by practice-oriented professional literature, containing applied theory and methods for the many specializations in social work. In fact, most social workers with a diploma or bachelors degree gain(ed) the bulk of their theoretical and methodological knowledge in this form.

By taking the different subjects outlined in the international definition of social work as a reference (see Section 1.1), and by relying upon the most well-known approaches and theories of social work textbooks, the following approaches and theories form the main areas of the body of knowledge of social work:

- Humanistic Psychology, with Maslow and his motivation theory as the most significant representative.

- Holistic Approach, as a significant characteristic of social work, according to IFSW as well as many authors and social workers.

- Ecological Systems Theory of developmental psychologist Urie Bronfenbrenner.

- Theory of Communicative Action: Life World and System World (Habermas).

- Planned Change Theory.

Besides these well-known, widespread approaches and theories, there are many others used in social work, such as anti-oppressive, radical, educational, and gender specific approaches and theories. Most of them, however, are less known, and have a limited scope because of their specific, context bound, premature or otherwise limited character. New, promising approaches are 'Constructive social work' (Parton and O'Byrne 2000) and 'Integrative theories', like the one of Donkers (2010) that I discuss in Section 3.4.5.

Contained below is a brief description of five well-known and important knowledge components of social work: their content and application are described in greater detail in Chapter 2.

1.4.1 Humanistic psychology

Because social work is based on humanitarian and democratic ideals, social workers are concerned with human welfare and social reform. They are keen on accommodating needs, and developing human potential. Therefore, the use of need and motivation theories provided by humanistic psychology is obvious. This branch in psychology tries to exceed the limitations of depth psychology (man as determined by unconscious motivations) and of behaviourism (influencing behaviour by rewards and punishment) by developing an approach in which man is considered as the holder of endless possibilities. By focusing on an overarching approach, as opposed to the single facets of attempting to manage the unconscious or viewing humans as being led by only reward and punishment, one can better explore human potential.

Humanistic psychology includes several approaches to counselling and therapy. The aim of humanistic therapy is to help the client develop a stronger and more healthy sense of himself or herself, also called self-actualization. Other well-known methods used in social work are gestalt therapy, encounter groups, sensitivity training, marital and family therapies, and, of course, the client-centred therapy of Carl Rogers. Also, co-counselling (as a self-help approach) is utilized in social work.

The developmental theory of Abraham Maslow, emphasizing a hierarchy of needs and motivations (Maslow 1943, 1987; Maslow and Lowery 1998), belongs to the body of knowledge of almost all social workers. In Maslow's theory, people's behaviour is very much led by satisfying needs. Maslow identifies five needs that lead in ascending order to the stadium of 'self-actualization': biological and physical needs, safety needs, belongingness and love needs, esteem needs, and finally self-actualization.

1.4.2 Holistic approach

The 'universal holistic focus' of social work (IFSW 2000, p.2) lies in the complex interaction between clients and their social environment, concerning different aspects of everyday life and on various scales. Change-oriented interventions by a social worker and/or client can only be effective if problems are analysed and handled in their mutual dependency and with regard to their specific nature.

In his article, 'Toward a common paradigmatic home: Social work in the 21st century', Richard Ramsay (1999) confirms the holistic focus of social work on the interaction between individual being and social environment. According to the author, this has been a central element in the body of knowledge of social work that has placed it at the head of the social sciences for many years. Ramsay praises social work for this feat:

> The recognition by social work pioneers of complex person-in-environment systems, and their intuitive sense of a holistic, deep ecological worldview shows them to be conceptual thinkers well ahead of their time. The value of their early insights has had to wait for an acknowledged science paradigm to emerge and receive public acceptance.

1.4.3 Ecological Systems Theory

Understanding the complex interaction between the individual and his social environment is the object of all social sciences, especially sociology, anthropology, psychology, and economics. One of the most influential and useful theories remains the Ecological Systems Theory of Urie Bronfenbrenner (1994). Viewed as a leading scientist in the field of developmental psychology, Bronfenbrenner successfully defended a new concept of 'development' in direct opposition to the classical school of psychological thought. He defines 'development' as the developing conception of an individual in his ecological environment, his relation to that environment, and the individual's capacity to discover, change, or retain the qualities of that environment.

Whether or not social scientists are willing to provide Bronfenbrenner with theoretical credit, elements of his Ecological Systems Theory are used in many forms and variations in social work publications.

1.4.4 Communicative action: Life World and System World

It is through communication that people interact, (mis)understand one another, construct realities, and/or change those realities if necessary or desired. Training in communication is therefore an important part of social work education.

Most clients of social workers are in a vulnerable, dependent position. Social workers are often confronted with (mis)communication in relationships between people having unequal positions and differences in power and wealth.

When differences in power and dependence are involved, and the communication and/or the context in which it occurs is dominated by one of the actors (an individual, a group, an organization, or an institution), social workers need a framework to understand what is happening in order to find solutions and help clients to cope with the situation.

Such a framework is offered by Jürgen Habermas (1981), representative of the Frankfurter Schule on the Theory of Communicative Action. This theory is driven by a belief in the power of reason, embodied in universal pragmatics and guided by inter-subjective recognition of three valid claims: truth, rightness and sincerity.

According to Houston (2009), 'communicative action occurs when two or more individuals reach a consensual understanding on goals and actions. This form of speech acts as a coordinating mechanism facilitating the expression of all three validity claims and reasoned argument' (p.15).

In reality, it is challenging to achieve such a situation when actors take different positions with competing interests in mind. Social workers know and recognize this very well. In his analysis, Habermas identifies two core spheres: the Life World and the System World. Although they join together in practice, they can be separately analysed, which will be the subject of Section 2.5.

1.4.5 Planned Change Theory

To influence the interaction between clients and their social environment, social workers use a wide range of skills, techniques, and methods on various levels. According to the IFSW, 'social work interventions range from primarily person-focused psychosocial processes to involvement in social policy, planning and development' (IFSW 2000, p.2).

Efforts of social workers are directed toward goal-oriented change of behaviour of persons, groups, organizations, and institutions in society, with collective and individual well-being as the final objective. For planning and support of change processes, social workers make use of Planned Change theories and problem-solving models.

Planned change is discussed in Chapter 3. I explain the theory and relate it to problem-solving models, interventions, methods, and strategies. As most social workers do, I consider the Theory of Planned Change as a panoply of instruments and techniques to initiate and support change processes in addition to one or more of the normative approaches that are common in social work. I also pay attention to current theoretical developments by discussing the outlines of a new integrative approach, stimulated by the revival of holism in social sciences. In this respect I discuss Gerard Donkers' new integrated theory of changing based on the concept of self-regulation.

1.4.6 Tasks, roles, and functions in society

According to the IFSW (2000, p.1) interventions in social work include 'counselling, clinical social work, group work, social pedagogical work, and family treatment and therapy' as well as efforts to facilitate people with the things they require to cope with their situation and/or to solve their problems. The interventions of social work also include 'agency administration, community organization and engaging in social and political action to impact social policy and economic development' (IFSW 2000, p.2).

The many tasks and roles of social work in various fields for different groups of clients are ordered and embedded in their professional context in Chapter 4.

The position and functions of social work in society are the subject of Chapter 5, in which I also discuss and clarify the mutual dependencies between social problems, social infrastructure, social work, social policy, and citizen participation.

Drawing 1 The social worker with tool box, global ideals and tasks (helping people to fit in society, as a piece in the puzzle) (© Henny Feijer)

2.

Surviving – Needs and Social Conditions

As described in the international definition, social work is focused on the interaction between the individual and his or her social environment. In practice, the profession makes use of system and behaviour theories from social sciences to better understand the social realities that social workers are confronted with, whether directly or indirectly (via their clients).

Well known and frequently used theoretical concepts and models in social work originate from Humanistic Psychology, Developmental Psychology, Ecological Systems Theory, and the Theory of Communicative Action. Key concepts from these models are: fulfilment of needs, self-realization, life conditions, and power and dependency. Also important is the interaction between these components, and the influence on communication between individuals, groups, organizations, and institutions.

In this chapter I work through these well-known fundamentals within the body of knowledge of social work. I explore their significance within social work practice: a practice characterized by a holistic approach of reality in which these models and concepts are used by social workers to support their clients. As a practical summary, the last section (2.6) contains a basic step-by-step description of social work.

2.1 Unequal chances

If you are born in a wealthy, developed country, you have at least 18 years to mature and become an 'adult'; that is, to become a citizen with all the rights and duties that come with it. This was not always the case. Late in 18th century Europe, interest and concern began to grow regarding specific needs and circumstances that children were facing. This lasted until well into the 20th century, before the 'right to be a child' was generally accepted and realized in all its worth. This was the case at least in wealthy, developed countries.

If you are born in a prosperous country, most of the time the cradle, clothes, toys, and the baby room are already waiting for you as soon as you come home from the hospital. Additionally, social, medical, and educational services are available for you as soon as they are needed. Babies from affluent countries are protected and sheltered from before their birth, and land, literally and metaphorically, in a 'made-up bed'. In many countries, however, this is not the case. How you are born, if and how well you are fed, sheltered, and cared for, how long your childhood lasts, and how great your chances are of a successful education and career all depend on your individual circumstances.

At the beginning of the 21st century, countries including Sweden, Germany, France, the Netherlands, Canada, and Australia are trendsetters in many respects. Administration, health care, education, and social care, in various ways, are taking into account the succession of life stages, from infant, to toddler, child, and adolescent, to adult and elderly. There are many special provisions, services, and regulations for children of all ages, as there are for adults of all ages. Parents with young children have tax reductions and can apply for all sorts of allowances and subsidies. Working parents are also entitled to maternity leave and parental leave.

In rich, developed countries, a single human life is of relatively high value; important enough to invest in it, and spend a substantial amount of money to save, heal, or improve it. In countries such as the Netherlands, Germany, and Sweden, more than half of the gross national product is spent on the collective sector. This includes environmental infrastructure, safety, social security, education, health care, social care, and various financial supports for citizens with special needs, as well as the administration involved in planning and implementation.

Because these countries are constitutional states with a parliamentary democracy, a free press, and civil rights, the possibilities for corruption are limited; public means are generally spent on what they are meant for. Citizens of these countries actually see and experience the benefits and returns for the taxes and premiums they pay. This is an important fact, because it stimulates acceptance and the willingness to pay taxes, and provides support for public institutions and services. This is in the interest of all, because everyone makes use of public services and supports at some point in their lives. Unfortunately, not all people live in countries with such resources. There is still a vast amount of inequality and injustice in the world, despite the Universal Declaration of Human Rights, despite the accumulation of wealth in many countries, and despite the availability of advanced technology to create liveable circumstances for all people in the world.

A stallholder at a market in India, with whom I discussed the differences between his country and mine, summarized our discussion as follows: 'You are lucky that you are born in the Netherlands.' However, this is only a part of the truth. Social inequality not only exists *between* countries, but also *within* countries, no matter whether the country is wealthy or poor. In almost all countries in the world, it (still) impacts individuals if they are born a child of lower class, middle class, or higher class parents. Social descent is an important influencing factor for a child's chances of success in life.

But everything is relative, including wealth and poverty. Because the standard of living can vary widely between countries, the life circumstances of a poor citizen in a wealthy, developed country look very different from the poverty experienced by a poor citizen of an impoverished, less developed country.

2.2 Needs and desires

There are notable differences and similarities between humans. An essential similarity is that we are all of the same biological species, constructed in the same way. To survive, people must fulfil basic needs for oxygen, water, food, shelter, clothing, sleep, sex, and reproduction. However, a human being is more than purely a biological entity. Humans have a conscience and a personality, and are also relational and spiritual beings. These unique human characteristics demand that needs beyond the basics must also be met in order to live a humane life.

2.2.1 Hierarchy of Needs

According to Abraham Maslow, an exponent of the Humanistic School of Psychology, the fulfilment of needs motivates people to act, to develop behaviour, and to construct and maintain organizations. Maslow first published his Hierarchy of Needs in 1943 in an article for *Psychological*

Review, entitled 'A Theory of Human Motivation'. In 1954 he published his book *Motivation and Personality*.

Maslow distinguishes between five different types of needs, and places them in an ascending order. The lowest level is that of biological and physiological needs. This is followed by the need for safety, then belonging and love needs. Esteem needs are next, and on the highest level is the need for self-actualization. In his later work, Maslow referred to additional needs of cognitive and aesthetic character, and to 'transcendence' as a higher form of self-actualization (Maslow and Lowery 1998). Although Maslow did not extend his own model with these three needs, there were others who did.

Figure 2.1 Hierarchy of Needs (based on Maslow 1954)

1. The needs on the lowest level are known as *biological and physiological needs*. They include the fulfilment of fundamental needs to survive, such as oxygen, hydration, food, clothes, shelter, sleep, and sex. If these needs cannot be satisfied sufficiently, existence is endangered and development toward higher levels of satisfaction is blocked.

2. *Safety needs* are needs for protection, security, order, law, limits, and stability. They concern the creation and presence of 'basic

trust', crucial in childhood for development of self-confidence as well as trust in others in later stages of life.

3. The level of *belongingness and love needs* encompasses giving and receiving love and affection, understanding, and acceptance. Individuals need to identify with a group in order to feel as though they belong. Such a group could be one's family, friends, peers, co-workers, or simply a group of people that an individual can identify with and relate to. Membership of a group allows an individual to feel a sense of belonging, as well as an opportunity to practise appropriate social behaviour.

4. *Esteem needs* are associated with self-confidence, appreciation by others, and the desire for freedom and independence. Key concepts are: respect, acceptance, recognition as a person, recognition of qualities, prestige, and acquiring a position in a group to which one belongs or wants to belong. Self-esteem is fundamental in establishing the ability to appreciate others. To satisfy esteem needs, there are also specific cognitive needs (learning, exploring, discovering) to fulfil, as well as aesthetic needs (creativity and beauty in all its natural and cultural forms).

5. On the highest level, *self-actualization* is the desire to reach one's fullest potential and to actually achieve that potential. It is an instinctual need to make the most of your abilities. If lower needs are satisfied, an individual can develop fully without feeling pressure to fight for a position, free from fear of the disapproval of others. Based on the achieved self-esteem, one can realize his or her full potential. This opens one up to a possible state of transcendence, meaning exceeding the boundary of common observation or consciousness, going beyond oneself. One comes to realize that the external world, as it appears, is not the only truth, but is based on a deeper reality, where one's own self is also based. Transcending occurs in many forms and on various levels.

With modifications, Maslow's Hierarchy of Needs is still valid today. It helps, for example, with the raising of children, and contributes to a greater understanding of their development toward maturity. It is also useful for motivation and further development of adults in the various stages of their lives.

At the basic level, children are provided with regular nourishment and care. On the second level, self-reliance and trust in others is formed through having safety, security, order, and stability in a child's care. The third level is about belonging, love, acceptance of the child, and identifying with groups. At the fourth level, experiencing success and independence is important, at school as well as at home. These four levels are necessary to ascend to the higher level, which has the potential to be realized in adulthood.

The lowest four levels of needs are characterized by Maslow as *deficiency motivators*, whereas the needs on the highest level are *growth needs*. According to Maslow, only a small percentage of mankind will reach the highest level of self-actualization and transcendence. Most people will remain on the lower levels of the hierarchy of needs. As long as people have to struggle to maintain or recover self-confidence and need fulfilment, they will have less energy to use for developing abilities and skills to reach their fullest potential.

Thanks to increasing wealth, and the growing number of prosperous countries, more people than ever before are reaching higher levels of satisfaction and fulfilment. As a result, there is a growing interest in and need for self-development, through spirituality, creativity, and arts. People's focus has shifted from the external world to the internal world, within themselves. As such, individual enjoyment and positive experiences become values, and fit well in the ongoing process of individualization around the world.

Maslow's Hierarchy of Needs is neither complete nor exhaustive. Nevertheless, it is a clear, recognizable, useful, and workable model for understanding, explaining, facilitating, steering, and managing human behaviour on various levels, in different fields, and in many situations, especially also for social workers.

2.2.2 Motivation theories

Maslow's Hierarchy of Needs is a well-known, frequently used model, not only in social work, but also in organization psychology, public administration, business administration, and management studies. For this reason it is not by coincidence that in these fields especially, the development of motivation theories has continued.

Marcel Nieuwenhuis (2012) gives a clear overview of contemporary motivation theories. According to him, 'motivating employees is a very complex and not fully understood psychological issue. In modern psychological theory, classical thinking has made room for a more integrated approach in which motivation from different angles is the object of research' (Nieuwenhuis 2012, p.1 translation WB). When it comes to motivating employees, the question is how motivated behaviour can be stimulated, strengthened, maintained, reduced, and extinguished. According to Nieuwenhuis, it essentially concerns the conditions which stimulate employees to become and stay self-driven and competent. He describes the most important contemporary contributions to the needs and motivation theories through four different approaches:

- *Personal qualities approach.* Authors including Miller and McClelland focus on the personality of the employee. Which underlying personal qualities and motives determine the creation and continuation of motivation?

- *Outcomes approach.* Vroom and Adams concentrate on the expectations of employees toward contributions and outcomes. The motivation will rise if employees expect that their efforts will result in the desired outcomes.

- *Goal approach.* An employee can be motivated by setting goals that are clear, accepted, feasible, and challenging. Based on this assumption, Bandura designed his Goal Setting Theory, and Skinner developed his Theory of Behaviour Modification.

- *Tasks approach.* Authors including Deci and Hackman and Oldham put emphasis on the content of the tasks of the employee. Tasks are crucial in the motivation of employees to participate in an activity. The research is focused on autonomy, competence, and individual responsibility. (Nieuwenhuis 2010, p.130)

Figure 2.2 gives an overview of these four contemporary approaches of needs and motivation.

The different approaches can be described as follows (summary of an overview by Nieuwenhuis 2010, pp.131–141):

Characteristics: Miller and McClelland

In the SIMA-approach (System for the Identification of Motivation Aptitude) of Miller, motivational, natural talents of an employee are identified, with emphasis on their manifestation and application. It is all about what an employee, deliberately or not, strives for in his work. The motivation pattern, as a result, is the basis for the employee's behaviour. Working with behaviour patterns places demands on management and communication, taking natural talents as a starting point. McClelland takes four core motivators as the starting point: power, performance, attachment, and avoidance. If one of these motives dominates, it will have definite results on preferred activities. For example, someone who is attracted to power seeks power situations. It is essential first to know what motivates people, and then connect them with appropriate work based on their available natural talents.

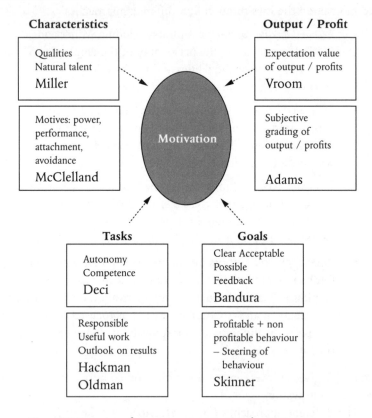

Figure 2.2 Overview of contemporary motivation theories in management (based on Nieuwenhuis 2010, translated by W. Blok)

Expectations of output: Vroom and Adams

This approach is aimed at motivational aspects of change. In the motivation model of Vroom – the Expectancy Theory – motivation is determined by the 'expectation' that work leads to a specific 'output' with a certain 'value in the form of a profit'. Based on these expectations, the employee makes an effort. Employees are motivated to perform and continue their job if their expectation leads to the desired results/profit. It is necessary to make and keep the relationship between efforts and output clear, with communication as an important factor for doing so.

The Equity Theory of Adams is similar to Vroom's theory. Where Vroom names output and contributions in more objective terms, Adams emphasizes the subjectivity of observations. Subjective views measure the total amount of contributions, and results/output are considered as fair or reasonable by a person. An employee may be satisfied with the balance between contribution and output. However, upon comparison with the results/output of a more experienced or productive colleague, initial satisfaction can change into dissatisfaction.

Goal setting: Bandura and Skinner

The setting of goals, as in Bandura's Goal Setting Theory, and management by objectives as predecessor, are commonly accepted approaches in everyday practice. Individuals must begin with the setting of concrete and clear goals. These goals have to be accepted by all parties involved. Goals need to be challenging and difficult, but not impossible to realize. It is also necessary to keep employees informed about the achievement of the goals that have been set. Feedback is vital as long as it is constructive and given at the appropriate times. This is especially true at moments in which changing or modifying behaviour is possible and productive.

A more clinical variant is Skinner's Behaviour Modification Theory. Briefly, the principle is that profitable behaviour is repeated, and non-constructive behaviour is avoided. Research has shown that intermittent rewarding of behaviour has the most powerful effect. For example, giving a reward in half of the cases is likely to be more effective than giving a reward in every instance.

Content of the task: Deci, Hackman and Oldham

This category of concepts and theories concentrates on the content of the tasks. According to Deci, work must meet two criteria in order to motivate an employee: it has to foster autonomy and the employee must be competent. This means that an employee takes on the most important decisions and responsibilities associated with his task, relative to his ability and competency. If a worker is given leeway to act, and has the proper skills and abilities, the employee will be intrinsically motivated to continue his work.

In the motivation model of Hackman and Oldham the leading principle is that employees are more motivated in their work if they are personally responsible for it, if they consider their work to be valuable, and if they have foresight into the end results. In practice, this model is effective in steering processes of task enrichment. Greater autonomy and better feedback regarding outcome, combined with emphasis on the importance of the job, stimulates the motivation of employees.

This overview of Nieuwenhuis (2010, pp.131–141) clarifies that motivation of people can be stimulated in many different ways, based on different approaches. Although the described theories are all related to work situations, with people in the roles of employee and employer, they are also useful in the field of social work and related professions. Social workers often deal with clients facing disappointment, dissatisfaction, and despair. In one way or another, these clients must be supported and empowered to find and generate motivation, to set new goals in life, and to change their patterns of thinking and behaviour in order to approach problems in a more effective manner.

2.2.3 16 basic needs

In many psychological theories on motivation, a distinction is made between intrinsic motivation and extrinsic motivation. Intrinsic motivation means that the motivation to do something comes from inside a person. Extrinsic motivation means that the motivation, or pressure to do something, comes from outside the person (e.g. from an individual's partner, parents, teacher, employer, or a police officer).

This long-established distinction in psychology is criticized by Steven Reiss as cited in an article by De Bruin (2005) 'A typical intrinsic motivation as curiosity for example, can also be evoked by the social environment,' according to Reiss, 'because people in boring circumstances are going to explore other realities by themselves.' He also criticizes the idea that intrinsically motivated behaviour is seen as an outcome, while extrinsically motivated behaviour is seen as a means to achieve something else, such as money or status. According to Reiss, a means can never compete with a goal: means facilitate goals, while someone can also be intrinsically motivated to earn money.

Reiss conducted studies involving more than 10,000 open and anonymous interviews with people in the USA, Canada, and Japan, across cultural borders. He found that a limited number of basic desires guide nearly all meaningful behaviour.

Reiss published his findings in *Who am I? 16 Basic Desires That Motivate Our Actions and Define Our Personalities* (Reiss 2000). The 16 basic desires are:

- *Power*, desire to have influence
- *Curiosity*, need for knowledge
- *Independence*, desire for autonomy
- *Status*, need for social recognition and attention
- *Social contact*, need for company and playing
- *Vengeance*, need to break even, but also to fight and to win
- *Honour*, need to obey traditional moral standards and values
- *Idealism*, need to improve society and being altruistic and righteous
- *Physical exercise*, need to train the muscles
- *Romance*, need for sex and courtship
- *Family*, desire to raise children
- *Order*, need to organize and perform rituals
- *Eating*, need for food
- *Acceptance*, need for acknowledgement
- *Tranquility*, need to avoid unrest and fear
- *Saving*, need to collect and to economize.

According to Reiss these desires drive our everyday actions and make us who we are. At least 14 of the 16 basic desires seem to have a genetic basis (they are similar to those seen in animals). Only the desires for idealism and acceptance do not.

On an individual level, one can see varying combinations of needs and desires. Religious people scored high on 'honour' and 'family', and low on 'vengeance' and 'independence'. Sports students scored high on 'physical exercise', 'social contact', 'family', 'vengeance', and 'power', and low on 'curiosity'. Students in secondary education with low grades scored low on 'curiosity', 'honour', and 'idealism', and high on 'vengeance' and 'social contact' (de Bruin 2005).

Today the Reiss Profile is used in various fields and situations. According to Step4ward, Institute for the Reiss Profile (2011), 'competence-based human resources consulting with the aid of the Reiss Profile' is offered in the following domains:

- personnel selection
- personnel development
- personality development
- organizational development
- team development
- outplacement
- behaviour training
- coaching.

Because these fields are related to or overlap with social work, the use of the Reiss Profile in social work can be effective as a diagnostic instrument, a tool for self-knowledge, and as an indicator for behavioural change.

2.3 The 'whole' human being

The existence of different levels of needs reveals that human beings are versatile. More precisely, man is a physical, mental, rational, social, and spiritual being. In health care and social work, we speak about man in this context as a *psychosociosomatic being*. Connecting the words *psycho*, *socio*, and *somatic* demonstrates that individual problems, deficiencies in society, and illnesses have multiple causes as well as multiple effects on individual beings, and most of the time they need multiple solutions. This is called a 'holistic' approach.

2.3.1 Holism

'Holism' and 'holistic' originate from the Greek word *holon*, meaning whole, entirety, or completeness. Holism is a way of thinking in which the whole is seen as a separate entity, consisting of constituent parts (or components) but not as the sum of them. The constituent parts affect each other and, by doing so, create a unique, separate entity.

The Swedish psychologist David Magnusson (2000) describes how the holistic approach is basically rooted in the history of scientific psychology. In the early part of the twentieth century, 'a holistic position was strongly advocated, from different perspectives, by some of the most distinguished psychologists, among them Gordon Allport, Alfred Binet,

Wilhelm Stern, Egon Brunswik, and Kurt Lewin' (Magnusson 2000, p.33).

In the 1950s and 1960s the holistic view was out of fashion in scientific psychology, as it was in other social sciences. The dominating behaviourism, the preference for experiments, the focus on natural sciences, and the strong emphasis on theoretical models at the micro level of individual functioning 'lacked a foundation in careful, systematic analyses of the character of the phenomena under investigation, and were not formulated within a common, integrated theoretical framework for individual functioning and development' (p.34). The end result was, according to Magnusson, 'compartmentalization and fragmentation of psychological theorizing and empirical research' (p.34).

The main cause of this fragmentation in psychology is, in Magnusson's view, 'the absence of a holistic integrated model for individual functioning and development, which could serve as the common theoretical framework for theorizing and empirical research on psychological phenomena.' But there was a problem, namely:

> The traditional holistic view was empty; it lacked specific content about the functioning and interplay of basic psychological and biological elements operating in the processes of the integrated organism. What went on between the stimulus and the response was regarded as unknown and inaccessible to scientific inquiry. (Magnusson 2000, p.34)

In recent decades, an increasing number of voices have been raised in support of this neglected perspective. In 1979, Robert Cairns formulated a view of developmental processes that is still utilized currently. He summarized his view as follows: 'Behavior, whether social or nonsocial, is appropriately viewed in terms of an organized system, and its explanation requires a "holistic analysis"' (cited in Magnusson 2000, p.34).

The holistic approach in scientific psychology developed slowly in the 1980s by gaining some influence on theory and empirical research dealing with central concepts such as perception, cognition, and memory. Since the 1990s, the holistic approach in social sciences has developed more rapidly. In psychology, pioneering developments in applied fields have generated a solid theoretical foundation for planning, implementation, and interpretation of empirical research on specific problems.

According to Magnusson, 'four main sources have contributed to this by enriching the empty holistic view with substantive content and providing methodological tools and research strategies which are compatible with the nature of the phenomena with which we are concerned' (p.35). These four main sources are:

- research on mental (or cognitive) processes

- research on biological aspects of individual development and functioning

- modern models for dynamic complex processes

- longitudinal research.

Research on mental processes

For a long time mental processes were neglected in psychology. But since the 1960s 'research on information processing, memory, and decision making has made dramatic progress and contributed essential knowledge necessary for the understanding and explanation of individual development and functioning' (Magnusson 2000, p.35). Magnusson strongly believes that if these concepts are extended to include emotions and values, they will closely resemble a holistic theoretical framework for future research.

Research on biological aspects of individual development and functioning

Medicine and biology have provided new insights into the role of internal biological structures and processes in the total functioning and development of individuals.

Research has shown 'how multiple brain regions, operating in synchronic interaction, are involved in complex perceptual-cognitive processes' (Magnusson 2000, p.36) This has helped to 'bridge the gap between biological and psychological models' (p.36), as that is also the case with the 'growing understanding of the role of biochemicals in the individuals way of dealing with situational-environmental conditions' (p.37).

Another valuable contribution of biology is the research on the role and influence of genes in individual development processes. 'The discovery of DNA and the genetic code in the 1960s (...) opened up new windows for mapping the individual genome structure and for research

on the mechanisms by which genetic factors operate in individuals.'
(p.38).

Modern models for dynamic complex processes

The third source for the application of a holistic perspective in psychology
is formed by the universal models developed in natural sciences for the
study of dynamic complex processes: Chaos Theory, General Systems
Theory, and Catastrophe Theory. 'These theoretical models, particularly
Chaos Theory, have had an almost revolutionary impact on both theory
building and empirical research in scientific disciplines that focus on
multidetermined stochastic processes such as meteorology, biology,
chemistry, and ecology', according to Magnusson (p. 38) He is of the
opinion that 'the way in which mental, biological, behavioral, and
social factors operate together in individual development and individual
functioning can be likened to a series of complex dynamic and adaptive
processes' (p.38).

In psychological research, the general systems approach is adopted,
and to a lesser degree the chaos and catastrophe theories. For Magnusson,
these modern models all emphasize the holistic, integrated nature of
dynamic, complex processes. They also:

> provide a theoretical framework for understanding the dynamic
> processes of interaction of operating factors within the individual,
> and the continuous bidirectional interaction between the individual
> and his or her environment in the person-environment system,
> within a single integrated perspective. Interaction among operating
> factors is a fundamental characteristic of the processes at all levels
> of the dynamic, integrated person-environment system. (Magnusson
> 2000, p.39)

Longitudinal research

The fourth and main source of enrichment for the holistic perspective lies
in the revival of longitudinal research. 'Inadequacies of the piecemeal or
variable oriented approach to the study of developmental issues become
obvious in well-planned longitudinal studies that track individuals
over time and contexts' (pp.40–41). Magnusson is of the opinion that
this longitudinal design is necessary for understanding developmental
processes.

For psychologists such as Magnusson, the ultimate goal is to understand and explain thoughts, feelings, actions, and reactions of individuals. One of his conclusions is that

> any general model which seeks to contribute to this goal must incorporate mental, biological, behavioural, and social factors into a single integrated model. These factors function simultaneously and need to be placed in a coherent theoretical framework, in which the total individual is the organizing principle. That is, any general framework for psychological research must be holistic. (Magnusson 2000, p.42)

Thus far, Magnusson is satisfied with the outcome: 'The modern holistic-interactionist view offers a stable platform for further scientific progress in psychology, enabling us to fall into step with recent developments in other disciplines in the life sciences' (p.42).

Magnusson is an advocate of Developmental Science. This new science is multidisciplinary because 'it is located at the interface of developmental psychology, developmental biology, molecular biology, physiology, neuropsychology, social psychology, sociology, anthropology, and neighboring disciplines' (p.42).

To stimulate and institutionalize this new science, a Center for Developmental Science was erected in 1994 at the University of North Carolina in Chapel Hill. Robert Cairns was the founding director of the Center, and served in this position until his death in 1999. Today, the Center for Developmental Science (CDS) (2012) has six strategic research objectives:

1. To serve as an inter-institutional and interdisciplinary institute of advanced study in human development.

2. To enhance teaching by providing an advanced interdisciplinary studies programme in developmental science for undergraduates, doctoral students, postdoctoral fellows, visiting scholars, and affiliated faculty members.

3. To foster and support student and faculty scholarship and research collaboration across disciplines, departments, schools, and universities in the study of developmental processes. A special emphasis is placed on involving early-career scientists in collaborations that will help them in developing their own research programmes.

4. To foster cross-institutional cooperation in developmental studies at component campuses of the University of North Carolina, private universities in North Carolina, and other US and international institutions.

5. To advance the frontiers of behavioural, biological, and social science by supporting interdisciplinary research and training on the bio-behavioural development of individuals over their lifespan and across generations.

6. To serve society by establishing linkages between the University of North Carolina, the state, the nation, and the world through research related to the promotion of health and well-being in individuals, families, schools, and communities.

Today the CDS is still flourishing. The Center is embedded in a faculty consisting of scientists of six universities and has a select group of researchers. At this moment CDS has three branches: the Carolina Consortium on Human Development, the Behavioral Science Research Division, and the Social Development Research Division.

2.3.2 Holistic interactionism

Magnusson presents a theoretical framework that he calls holistic interactionism. He describes the reason for developing it as follows:

> A modern holistic view emphasizes an approach to the individual and the person-environment system as organized wholes functioning as integrated totalities. At each level, the totality derives its characteristic features and properties from the interaction among the elements involved, not from the effect of each isolated part on the totality. Each aspect of the structures and processes that are operating (perceptions, plans, values, goals, motives, biological factors, conduct, etc.), as well as each aspect of the environment, takes on meaning from the role it plays in the total functioning of the individual. (Magnusson 2000, pp.42–43)

The role of the acting individual, essential for social work, is tied in with Magnusson's concept of 'self-organization'. 'Self-organization is a characteristic of open systems and refers to a process by which new structures and patterns emerge. From the beginning of fetal development, self-organization is a guiding principle in developmental processes' (p.43). Magnusson quotes Nobel laureate Jacob: 'Finality in the living world thus originates from the idea of organism, because the parts have to produce each other, because they have to associate to form the whole, because, as Kant said, "living beings must be self-organized"'(p.44).

Magnusson's holistic interactionism fits with the body of knowledge of social work because of the wide, integrated approach of human behaviour, the interaction between the individual and his or her surroundings, the various roles played by actors, and the unique circumstances of each situation. Magnusson's approach provides the social worker with a wide and varying repertoire of interventions to support the change of behaviour of clients and surrounding actors in a desired direction.

What does not complement social work is the absence of the responsible individual, the responsible citizen with rights and duties, who, if necessary, can be called to accountability and carry the consequences for his or her own actions. In this respect, holistic interactionism and the concept of self-organization need further elaboration and explanation. And, of course, operationalization is necessary to generate applicable instructions that can be used in varying practices and situations.

Due to their orientation regarding the interaction between the individual and his surroundings (see Chapter 1), social workers are used to looking through holistic glasses at the everyday reality of their clients and themselves. This dates back to the beginning of the 20th century:

> Continuing the philosophy and efforts of social work legend, Mary Richmond, this holistic approach brings together a time tested perspective to social work blending individual, ecological, and systems theories and acknowledging the physical, mental, emotional, social, economic, cultural, and spiritual dimensions of human life. (Blachman 2004, p.217)

Its holistic approach is a distinctive characteristic of social work: 'Central to family health theory and practice is consideration of unique aspects of contemporary family life, such as neighborhood and culture, often overlooked by other practitioners of other clinical methods' (Blachman 2004, p.218).

John Murphy (1994) also concludes that a holistic approach is common among social workers. The individual is seen as more than an isolated psychological being, because he or she is influenced by social class, experiences, culture, and language through interaction with others. In the words of Murphy: 'The individual should be viewed as more than a psychological entity. Variables such as class, personal and collective experiences, language use, and styles of parental interaction, for instance, are to be viewed as shaping behavior' (p.56). He continues by saying: 'No person should be viewed as an island... Instead, behavior should be viewed as multidimensional and facts should be supplemented by evidence. As a result, data are reviewed in the proper perspective and assessed within the social context' (p.56).

Murphy is of the belief that holism within social work practice needs more theoretical foundation and legitimization, and connects it with elements of postmodernism. In my opinion, this is not a practical perspective. It makes more sense to connect to holistic approaches in social science and research, such as Magnusson's holistic interactionism described and discussed previously.

Based on the latest results of scientific research, the holistic approach has made a comeback in social sciences, in the form of new concepts and theories. If the revival of holism is as durable as it appears to be, it will generate a continuous stream of insights, concepts, and models that can be useful for social workers and related professionals, and that can extend and enrich the body of knowledge of social, medical, therapeutic, and educational professions. However, as in the case of social work, it is necessary to 'translate' theoretical insights, concepts, and models into practice-oriented standards, knowledge, and methods, meeting the unique needs of the specific professional fields.

Translation, adaptation, and operationalization are pre-eminently a task for the developers, researchers, and teachers of the many applied sciences, professional theories, and methodological courses developed, taught, and trained since the 1960s. This is also true for the social, medical, therapeutic, and educational professions. Most of the generated knowledge and skill is aimed at changing practical behaviour of individuals, groups, and organizations, simultaneously improving work and life conditions. I refer to Theory of Social Work, Theory of Education, Social Case Work, Group Dynamics, Pedagogic Help, Psychotherapy, Creative Therapy, Public Administration, Marketing, Community Development, Human Resource Management, Communication Theory, and various types of practice methods, orientations, courses, and training.

2.4 Life conditions: Ecological Systems Theory

Through continuous efforts to satisfy needs, develop skills, and increase knowledge, the individual depends on the environment which he is a part of. The ongoing interaction between person and environment is a multiple, mutual influencing process, in which many actors and factors (e.g. positions, roles, rules, possessions, and power balance) are involved.

To fully comprehend the complex interaction between a person and his or her environment, many social workers and related professionals rely on the concepts and insights of the Ecological Systems Theory of psychologist Urie Bronfenbrenner.

With his developmental concept of interaction and mutuality between individual person and environment, Bronfenbrenner (1979) broke through the biased emphasis of traditional developmental psychology on the individual being, and traditional sociology on the environment. Bronfenbrenner defined 'development' as the developing view of an individual person from his ecological environment, of his relation with it, and of his ability to discover, continue, or change it.

Based on this transactional approach of educational and developmental psychology and sociology, Bronfenbrenner constructed the Ecological Systems Theory. It is an open system approach that is similar to that of the holistic interactionism of Magnusson (see Section 2.3.2).

In the Ecological Systems Theory the individual is surrounded by five systems (Bronfenbrenner 1994), namely:

1. *The microsystem*

   Examples: family, siblings, schoolmates, peer group, neighbours.

   Definition: 'A pattern of activities, social roles, and interpersonal relations experienced by the developing person in a given face-to-face setting with particular physical, social, and symbolic features that invite, permit or inhibit engagement in sustained, progressively more complex interactions with, and activity in, the immediate environment' (p.1645).

2. *The mesosystem*

   Examples: neighbourhood, town, school, sports club, office, workplace.

   Definition: 'Comprises the linkages and processes taking place between two or more settings containing the developing person (e.g. the relations between home and school, school and workplace, etc.)' (p.1646).

3. *The exosystem*

   Examples: powerful institutions and structures with established standards and regulations.

Definition: 'Comprises the linkages and processes taking place between two or more settings, at least one of which does not contain the developing person, but in which events occur that indirectly influence processes within the immediate setting in which the developing person lives' (p.1646).

4. *The macrosystem*

   Example: the larger social-cultural context, such as the national state.

   Definition: 'Consists of the overarching pattern of micro, meso, and exosystems characteristic of a given culture or subculture, with particular reference to the belief systems, bodies of knowledge, material resources, customs, life-styles, opportunity structures, hazards, and life course options that are embedded in each of these broader systems. The macrosystem may be thought of as a societal blueprint for a particular culture or subculture' (p.1646).

5. *The chronosystem*

   Examples: changes over the life course in family structure, socioeconomic status, employment, place of residence, degree of busyness, and the ability to function in everyday life.

   Definition: 'Encompasses change or consistency over time not only in the characteristics of the person but also of the environment in which that person lives' (p.1646).

Due to the popularity of Bronfenbrenner's theory, many comprehensive diagrams were made to explain and teach his ecological model to students and workers. Figure 2.3 shows the one I use.

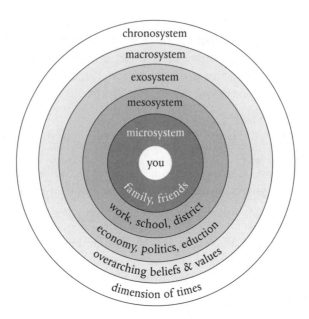

Figure 2.3 The Ecological Systems Theory (based on Bronfenbrenner 1994)

Within each of the systems, persons and groups are functioning in roles that are part of the informal or formal (e.g. institutional) settings of that system. Each system and setting produces and maintains standards and rules that influence life conditions and determine the possibilities and limitations for individuals to meet their needs and fulfil their desires.

In the Ecological Systems Theory, behavioural problems are not only of individual character, nor are they only caused by environmental influences. Behavioural problems are seen as a result of lacking balance in the individual eco system (e.g. as an interaction problem, a mismatch, between the individual and his environment).

Unbalance can be caused by a lack of commitment between individual expectations and those of the environment. However, it can also be the result of lack of coordination between different actors in the environment of the person in question.

To solve behavioural problems, changes are necessary. The actors involved are all in roles that are connected with a setting. Changes have the character of 'ecological transitions'. Such a transition takes place if the position of one or more persons changes due to a change in role, a change of setting, or both.

The question is: who and what has to change in order to solve the problem? The person with the problem? The persons who created the problem? The situation in the psychological and physical environment? Or the interaction between the various actors involved?

The Ecological Systems Theory still challenges and inspires professionals in many fields. It encourages breaking down barriers between sciences and professions, and building bridges between different disciplines. It is also useful as 'medicine' against fragmentation, isolation, and individualization. It can be considered a holistic approach, as in Magnusson's holistic interactionism (see Section 2.3.2).

The Ecological Systems Approach offers social workers the opportunity and means for a vast, open, and comprehensive approach to behavioural problems, and stimulates an interdisciplinary style of working. This opens a perspective toward more durable results in terms of better functioning clients in an improved environment.

2.5 Communicative action: Life World and System World

Communication is basic in human life. Nothing works without it. Appropriate, effective communication is therefore a challenge for everyone in society. Communication is an important factor in both the occurrence of problems and in solving them.

Effective communication is both a skill and an art. On a micro level it is part of the individual learning process that we call 'socialization'. On a meso level it helps people to understand each other, to cooperate, and to participate. On a macro level, communication sustains cultures, unites individuals, and gives them an identity, as well as keeping people informed of what is occurring around the world.

Hindering communication in any way creates misunderstanding, leads to questionable decisions, endangers relationships between people, causes conflicts, and generates problems. If a lack of communication or manipulated forms of communication draw people away from truth and reality, order can turn into chaos, and social responsibility can change into individual survival of the fittest.

Social workers are confronted, and have to cope with, inequalities between people. Most of the time, social work clients are vulnerable individuals and groups. Power, authority, and means are often the discriminating factors between people in a weak versus a strong position in society.

When it comes to something as challenging as communication, it is clear that communication between people in unequal positions is much more difficult than communication between equals. Social workers, dedicated to improving the position and situation of vulnerable people and groups in society, have a difficult job establishing effective forms of communication between powerful and vulnerable people. Quite often as a starting point, social workers have to act as mediators to bring people to, or keep people on, speaking terms.

On a theoretical level, communication can be better understood through communicative action. Jürgen Habermas (1981) gave birth to the Critical Theory, in which he defines communicative action as 'that form of social interaction in which the plans of action of different actors are co-coordinated through an exchange of communicative acts, that is, through a use of language orientated towards reaching understanding' (p.44). This can only be achieved if communication between different actors involved in a specific matter is based on truth, rightness, and sincerity, and on the inter-subjective recognition of these values by all parties involved. Habermas calls these *universal validity claims*.

In everyday reality, it is a challenge to create such a situation, especially between actors in different positions with different interests. Social workers are trained to understand and recognize this very well.

In his analysis of communicative action, Jürgen Habermas identifies two core spheres: the 'Life World' and the 'System World'. Although they are associated in practice, they can and should be analysed separately.

The Life World is the often overlooked universe of everyday existence, the saturation of communicative action by tradition and the way people are accustomed to doing things in their everyday lives.

The System World refers to areas of life that are organized and controlled by the state and the institutions in society, especially the political and economic subsystems that govern important aspects of our lives. 'Whereas the Life World is concerned with cultural integration and socialization, the System World focuses on material reproduction. Consequently, it is dominated by power, money and strategic action' (Houston 2009, p.16).

Problems occur when representatives of the Life World (citizens, interest groups) and System World (authorities, managers, officials) meet and interact, and one sphere dominates the other. These encounters happen worldwide on a daily basis, numerous times, and on micro, meso and macro levels.

In communicative action, participants coordinate their actions on the basis of a shared understanding that the goals they set are inherently reasonable or meritworthy. In contrast, strategic action is a form of action aimed to achieve particular ends, based on the use of influence, force, sanctions, or money. While communicative action is actually an inherently harmonious form of social coordination, strategic action is a form of fighting and competing for the best interest of a person, group, institute, or company. Without mediation, many interactions between Life and System Worlds are battle-grounds for strategic action from one or more sides, without the opportunity for communicative action from any actors involved.

Life World and System World have become more differentiated from each other, leading to a critical stage in society's development as we experience it today.

> Having uncoupled from the life world, the all-powerful system re-enters it, this time to colonize its functions. This means that instrumentality, rationality, money, bureaucracy and power – the trappings of the system – usurp communicative action as the chief means for resolving issues and problems in the life world. As a consequence, social life becomes increasingly monetarized, commodified and bureaucratized. In short, entropy sets in. An example of colonization is the bureaucratization of schools, where league tables and other performance criteria undermine the practice of education as a communicational discipline. (Houston 2009, p.17)

Habermas looks critically at the welfare state.

> By offering mainly bureaucratized interventions to those who are in need, it erodes earlier traditions of care, such as are found in neighborhoods and social networks, and also undermines the informal, communicational mechanisms that coordinate them. More than this, the system uses social welfare as a protective mechanism to ward off discontent in the life world. This occurs mainly when there are legitimation crises in the economy and the disparities between rich and poor become most acute. To offset the crisis, and mollify discontent, the welfare state provides social assistance and other benefits. (Houston 2009, p.17)

Modern history shows that parliamentary democracy, democratic action, and citizen participation are the best and most effective solutions to these kinds of developments. As long as authorities, institutes, and companies operate within the framework of a constitutional, democratic state, with a free press and respecting civil and human rights, they can be criticized, influenced, corrected, and directed by government and parliament.

In Chapter 5 I discuss the contribution of social work to democratic functioning of society on all levels and in all fields, by facilitating and supporting the participation of individual and organized citizens.

Houston (2009) concludes that there is a growing interest in Habermas' ideas in Western social work: 'For some commentators, his work provides a viable alternative to postmodernism, which, because of its perceived, inherent relativism, fails to offer the required justification for ethical practice'(p.19). Many social workers and social work researchers all over the world use concepts and elements of communicative action in their theoretical and methodical work in various fields; from decision making in fostering and adoption via family therapy, to working with mentally disabled, to care management in social work. On the meso and macro levels, Habermas' theory is very useful in practices such as user involvement, networking, action learning, and peer supervision.

2.6 Practice: the basics of social work

Motivation Theories (Section 2.2), Holistic Approach (Section 2.3), Ecological Systems Theory (Section 2.4), and Theory of Communicative Action (Section 2.5) are vital to the body of knowledge of social work as described in the international definition (Section 1.1). With the help of these fundamental theories it is possible to describe and explain the complex interaction between the individual being and his social environment in a clear, systematic way. This helps in understanding the origins of many problems, and offers starting points of action for social workers and other helping professionals in education, health care, and welfare.

I will outline this the way I do for students. I will begin 'from scratch' and construct a step-by-step approach that is fundamental for social work and other helping professions.

2.6.1 Nature and nurture

Each individual person is the product of two other human beings, a man and woman, whether conceived naturally or otherwise. A child bears the genetic mark of his biological parents.

If events after a child's birth go 'according to plan', the child's parent or parents (whether biological or not) will also take care of and nurture the child in and from the social group which they, therefore also their child, are a part of. However, various circumstances can cause things to occur very differently. In many situations, children are taken care of and raised by other family members, foster parents, or guardians, in and from the respective social group and culture to which the caregivers belong.

Figure 2.4 The individual person as member of a group

'Nature' (genes) and 'nurture' (socialization and education) have a strong influence on the first five or six years of a child's life. These early years greatly impact children and generate a 'blueprint' which affects how the child will grow up and find his way in life as an adult.

A child is greatly affected by his surroundings, but the opposite is also true; a child also influences other people in his environment. The very existence of the child has a great impact on the life conditions and behaviour of his or her parents or caregivers, and the people with whom they associate. These people must play new roles (such as father, mother, sister, grandparent, uncle, foster parent), fulfil the tasks related to those roles, and conduct themselves according to culturally determined rules of behaviour, law, and regulations for children and their caregivers. People are bound by the ties of caregiving for a period of at least 18 years, and have to adapt and alter their lifestyle and social activities accordingly.

The child itself, as part of a family, influences the others by his or her character, behaviour, and physical and mental condition. Family members are strongly connected, and are dependant on each other. Ideally, they develop long-lasting, reciprocal relationships based on mutual expectations, shared cultural standards and values, and specific behavioural patterns.

2.6.2 Social environment: micro, meso, and macro

Until school age, the child is raised in primary groups such as: family, day care centre, neighbours, and friends. These are groups on the *micro level* (from the Greek *mikros* = small), also named 'microsystem' in

(Ecological) Systems Theory. When the child grows up, he or she will also involve classmates in his or her direct environment.

School, neighbourhood, sports club, local government, supermarket, company, office, factory, local transport, and church are examples of institutes on the *meso level* (from the Greek *mesos* = middle) with which people deal on a regular, sometimes daily, basis. These establishments are important for meeting vital needs, (further) education, and socialization of children, adults, and the elderly.

Last, but not least, is the *macro level*, the larger social-cultural context, also in terms of the Ecological Systems Theory. An example on this level is the country a person lives in, is a citizen of, and of which that person speaks the language. Also on this level is the continent on which a person lives, the international authorities and institutes which a person's country is connected with, as well as the multinational organizations, companies, and services that influence the life circumstances of one's country, and the local area where a person lives.

To avoid confusion, I use the term 'level' to differentiate from the Ecological Systems Theory 'system'. For simplicity, I use three levels (micro, meso, and macro), while Bronfenbrenner uses five 'systems'. In the meso level I include both the 'mesosystem' (town, institutes, companies) as well as the underlying 'exosystem' (power and roles of the actors on meso level). I make no use of a separate 'chronosystem', but include the historical, developmental perspective in my analysis.

The social environment of an individual being can be visualized in Figure 2.5. The individual is in the centre. From his or her perspective, the various social groups, organizations, and institutes which the person is a part of or dependent on are placed on the level where the individual is functioning. The three levels, micro, meso and macro, are layers around the individual person. One can also imagine a set of Russian dolls, because the three levels are mutually connected and intertwined, as well as strengthening each other. The division between the levels is not intended as a total separation, but rather to demonstrate a distinction between the levels.

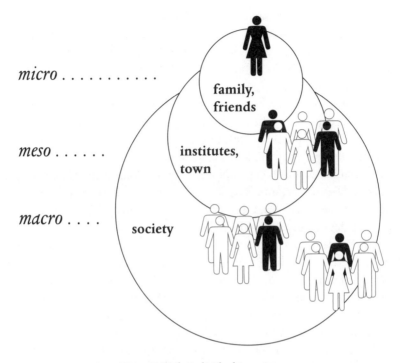

micro . . . .

meso . . . . . .

macro . . . .

Figure 2.5 The individual in society

Figure 2.6 Russian dolls

The neighbourhood or village where one lives (micro) is part of a municipality (meso) that is a part of the country, the national state (macro). The country is a member of multinational institutes (e.g. the European Union, NATO, and the United Nations) which are also part of the macro level.

An institute or event on the macro level seems distant, but under certain circumstances hits very close to home with its impact and consequences on the life conditions of social groups and individual persons. For example, think of a change in financial support for students, the social benefit of the unemployed, the pensions of the elderly, or the salaries of civil servants. The income of people is subject to national policy at the macro level, but effects are felt directly in the wallets of persons depending on that income.

In modern times, distance is relative. An incident with a nuclear plant in Russia can have negative effects on the natural environment in Western Europe. A terrorist attack in New York can have consequences for nations and people all over the world. Similarly, Chinese investments in poor countries can have positive effects on local employment and economic perspectives of ordinary citizens in those countries.

The hierarchical order of public institutions, and of (inter) national companies, crosses the boundaries of the different levels. A neighbourhood primary school is bound by policy and regulations of the national Ministry of Education, and the local supermarket is subject to regional, national, and international policy of the company that owns it.

The opposite is also true. A special event in a city, town, or village, or an extraordinary effort of a local person or regional institution, can attract national or international attention on the internet, television, radio, or newspaper, and can even have effects elsewhere in the world.

As in Bronfenbrenner's 'systems', on each of the three levels (micro, meso, and macro) various actors (an actor is an acting person, group, institute, company, or authority) play roles and perform tasks that are part of (institutional) settings. The cashier of the local supermarket checks the purchase of customers and collects the money. The policeman gives a fine for driving in the dark without proper lights. The teacher assigns grades. The British Prime Minister informs on cuts in the budget. The President of the USA proclaims the withdrawal of armed forces from Afghanistan, so that people's brothers, sisters or cousins will be home for Christmas. These examples demonstrate that actors and events on the macro, meso, and micro level are mutually connected, interact with each other continuously, and communicate both from the top down and the bottom up.

On each of the three levels, regulations and standards apply that (can) have a direct influence on the possibilities of the individual to satisfy his needs and improve his life conditions. In other words: if a person wants something, the individual will be directly or indirectly confronted with the existing possibilities and limitations of established structures and organizations, based on actual social relationships. To a certain extent, the individual is pressured to adapt to these in order to achieve or to keep what he wants.

2.6.3 Groups, structures, roles, and power

From the moment a child is born, he or she is a part of the social group of his or her parents or of the people who raise him. That social group is part of the society as a whole, existing on all three levels. Sociology demonstrates how people, based on the status of their education, profession, and wealth, place each other into groups ranging from high to low social classification.

Figure 2.7 shows how social stratification, the categorization of people in classes or strata, works.

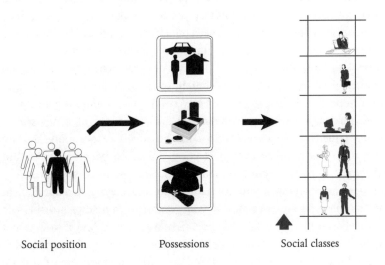

Social position   Possessions   Social classes

Figure 2.7 How social stratification works

Someone's social position is determined by his or her education and profession. How high the education, and how high the status and the earnings of the profession, determine how high the status and social position in society.

From childhood we learn to go along with others in and from certain roles. In daily life we play many roles, more than we realize, and often more than we can handle at the same time. For example: in the company of your parents you have the role of child, even if you are an adult, and together you form a family. You are also grandchild of grandmothers and grandfathers, of which you can have more than four in modern times. You are niece or nephew of the sisters and brothers of each of your parents, and cousins of their children. At school you are pupil, with classmates and teachers. If you go on studying, you will have the role of student and be attended by lecturers, tutors, and professors. You are friend of someone. You have the role of neighbour in the street where you live. At your work you are employee and you have colleagues, with chiefs and director in charge. In bus, tram, train, boat, or plane you are passenger. For the administration and the police you are citizen, holder of a residence permit, foreign tourist, or illegal person. If you commit a crime, you become suspect, and can be accused. If a judge agrees, you end up in a prison and become prisoner, guarded by warders. In health care you are patient. In social work and for a lawyer you are client. In the military you are soldier, sergeant, or officer. In (web)shops and the supermarket you are customer, as you are for the energy, gas, and water supplier. You are tenant if you rent a room or a house, and landlord or owner if a house or apartment is yours. You are member of many organizations: church, sports club, library, trade union, political party, self-help group, tenants' committee, welfare organization, or an association of dog owners. You are subscriber of a newspaper or magazine, listener or viewer for the broadcast corporation. You are voter and/or candidate during election time. You become driver, and participate in traffic, from the moment you step on or in a vehicle. At a congress or conference you are participant and maybe also speaker. In the stadium you are spectator. If you go abroad you step into the role of traveller, tourist, 'backpacker', or 'rich Westerner'. And if you earn a living from them, you work as pilot, hostess, driver, guide, tour leader, or hotel manager. And for this book I am author and you are (if you are still with me) reader.

Each role is part of a structure. Every structure generates different roles, and most of the time more persons are in the same role. Roles are played according to certain rules and regulations of behaviour. These rules and regulations are concrete expressions of the function and value of the role and the underlying structure according to the organization and the surrounding society (i.e. a big part of the population). If you are not (sufficiently) aware of it, you will be reminded by comments, complaints, sanctions, and punishment.

Examples: every citizen is expected to know the law. Drivers are expected to stop for a red traffic light. An owner of a restaurant is expected to prepare and serve food according to basic standards of hygiene. In many countries he is also obliged to forbid his customers to smoke. A surgeon is expected to have a proper education for what he is intending to do with his patient in the operating theatre. And from a politician in a democratic country we expect proper behaviour according to the law, and dedication to the public cause.

2.6.4 Abilities, attitude, and skills

On each of the three levels, micro, meso, and macro, people play roles and perform tasks in relation to others, both in their private lives and their public lives, within an organized institutional context. To fulfil roles and perform tasks in a way that satisfies others and oneself, certain mental and physical abilities are needed, as well as a vision of man's place in society, a belief system, and an appropriate attitude. Finally, a number of social and technical skills are necessary to successfully fill a role expectation.

The objective is to survive: to eat, have shelter, develop talents, and to build and maintain a way of life that is satisfying and fulfilling. In Maslow's terms, the goal is to meet the various needs outlined in the hierarchy of needs (see Section 2.2.1).

Figure 2.8 is a summary of an individual's three basic personal qualities, *abilities, attitude*, and *skills*, and how these affect one's capacity to fulfil certain roles. The five symbols on the left side of the outer circle represent basic needs and vital resources of every individual: *work (income), housing, education and development, environment*, and a *democratic state*.

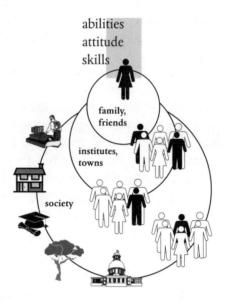

Figure 2.8 Individual and social conditions of a person

An individual must live with what he has, wherever he is, and from the very moment he arrives there. Every man must try to meet his own needs, regardless of the circumstances in which he finds himself. This requires great effort, whereby an individual must apply all that he has learned through his education and socialization.

What people have to offer differs from person to person. An individual who, by birth or by disease or accident, does not possess his full mental and/or physical abilities is in a weaker position than someone born with full capacity and capability who may simply be deemed more 'fortunate' in his life circumstances. This person's potential and chances of succeeding are likely to be much higher than those of the individual lacking specific abilities.

In a society where people compete for the best, where everything can be bought for a price, and where appearance and presentation are considered extremely important, a person with mental or physical challenges may be an 'underdog' by definition. Such a person is likely to require extra support and assistance to compensate for lack of certain capabilities.

Social circumstances differ between countries. A large portion of the world's population still struggles just to survive from one day to the next. This is not by choice, but is a result of the situation of their country, whether or not by its own doing.

2.6.5 Unsatisfied needs

Poor people, living in marginal social conditions who are not able to change their circumstances will usually reconcile themselves to their situation. Therefore, they will never reach a higher level of satisfaction in the hierarchy of needs as described by Maslow.

In the past, this would have been less troubling than today. Advanced, accessible telecommunications and mass transport have made the world 'smaller' than ever before in human history. Only in a few scattered instances do people today grow up and lead their lives in an isolated community. The implication is that people all over the world frequently, often on a daily basis, are confronted with images and sounds of people, life circumstances, religions, and habits from all over the world. Because of the huge commercial influence, television programmes advertise luxury goods and services, and promote a lifestyle whereby happiness is based on acquiring these things. This can be very disheartening for people who are not able to attain a Western life standard. The 'ignorance is bliss' of earlier times is no longer a reality in today's society.

If people cannot fulfil their needs in their environment, it will lead to disappointment, frustration, and dissatisfaction, depending on the extent to which their needs are not met. If people do not believe that change is possible, and lose hope for the future, the feelings of discontentment will only worsen.

In such situations people have a choice out of one of four reactions: fighting, fleeing, avoiding, or ignoring. If these unfortunate circumstances are sustained purposely by individuals, social groups, institutes, or companies who have a vested interest in doing so, the marginalized people have identifiable opponents. The exploited people then estimate the position and power of their opponents, then decide if it is possible to organize a successful collective resistance. This is what happened with the younger generations in many of the Arab countries, leading to the revolutions of 2011. If such a way out is unlikely, fleeing becomes the obvious choice, sometimes after a period of avoiding and/or ignoring.

These kinds of situations occur on all levels. On the world scale, people may flee their country; in families, teenagers revolt against parents; at work, a dissatisfied employee applies for another job, amongst many other possible scenarios. Besides the rather obvious responses such as fighting, fleeing, avoiding, or ignoring, there are also 'silent' reactions on a personal level in various forms, such as addiction (alcohol, drugs, gambling, and sex), stress, burnout, psychosomatic complaints like backache and headaches, stomach disorders, and food-related problems.

Figure 2.9 outlines these mismatches between individual needs and social conditions.

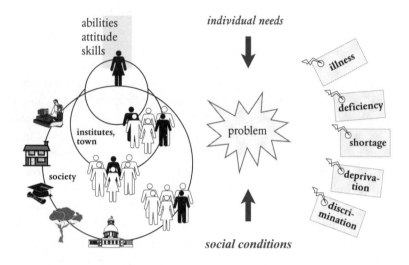

Figure 2.9 (Labelling of) mismatches between individual needs and social conditions

If a person cannot meet basic or vital needs in his or her environment, friction occurs between individual needs (demand) and (social) environment (supply). When the individual is not able to change this, and neither ignoring nor fleeing helps, the situation becomes problematic. The problems can vary in type and form, and may become persistent.

If a person seeks professional help, he or she will present his problem in terms of the specific discipline and practice of the consulted professional. Problems may be presented (and analysed) in the form of physical complaints to a doctor, as a mental disorder to a psychologist, as an offence or crime to the police, as legal issues to a lawyer, or as psychosocial problems to a social case worker. If other individuals have similar problems, they can be presented as collective or social problems to a sociologist, to a community worker, to a city council, or to a lawyer. Issues addressed by specific experts are 'diagnosed' based on initial assessment and analysis of the presenting problem. If the diagnosis falls under the realm of the professional's competency, the problem will be treated accordingly by that expert. If the diagnosis is beyond the expertise of that professional, the client will be referred to the appropriate specialist. In treatment, the person seeking help – the *problem owner* – is assigned a role respective to the discipline of the helping professional:

patient, client, victim, customer, or citizen. If the help is accepted, the individual is expected to behave according to the assigned role.

Labelling or diagnosing an individual's problem is a subjective activity between the person with the presenting problem and the helping professional. This is a critical moment in the helping process. There is a greater risk of 'self-fulfilling prophecy' (making things happen that you expect to see happening) if the diagnosis or analysis is not conducted according to professional standards, is inaccurate, or is incomplete.

If a problematic interaction between individuals and their environment becomes manifest in the form of physical and mental complaints, the involvement of various specialists may be necessary for a complete diagnosis and an appropriate, effective solution. In practice, this can not always be fully realized, and is definitely not 'automatic'. However, at present this is happening more often, because of a greater awareness and knowledge of the interaction between the individual and his environment. In other words, a holistic approach has become more common amongst professionals in health care, social work, and related fields. For this reason, there is more time and effort invested in coordination, cooperation, and interdisciplinary work than ever before.

Figure 2.10 shows the division of tasks developed, over time, between health care workers and workers in the three major fields of social work.

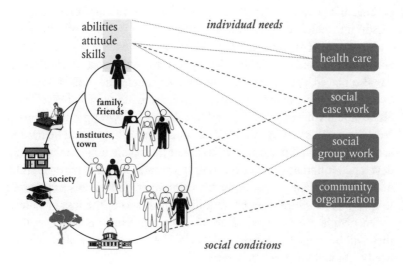

Figure 2.10 Division of tasks between health care and social care

Institutions and professionals in health care aim to alleviate or cure physical and mental ailments of people under their treatment and care. Social workers focus on the interaction between individuals and their environment. The social case worker practises face to face, in small groups on a micro level, and also partly on a meso level. The community worker and group worker are oriented to specific social groups, of (organized) citizens, resident groups, and day groups in institutions. These workers advocate for, facilitate, and support initiatives and actions to improve the everyday life situations of clients and citizens. They also empower their clients to have an influence on policy and functioning of institutes, public authorities, and the public opinion.

The column of professional fields on the right-hand side of the figure is in order of their occurrence in history. Their rise and success is more or less a result of the growing social awareness of social influence on mankind, and of the interaction between the individual and his environment. This is in accordance with the process of civilization and science, whereby social sciences appeared at the end of the 19th century and began blossoming after 1945.

2.6.6 Problem solving and compensation

If someone is not able to fulfil important needs in his social environment, he may be hampered in his development and could end up in a problematic situation. To solve, reduce, or prevent such problems, the person must take action, and if necessary, utilize the help of others (see Figure 2.11). This is no simple task. After all, even when an individual ends up in an undesirable situation against his will, most of the time he has also played a role in creating or contributing to the problem himself. Even when others may be mostly to blame, the individual always has at least some involvement in the problem, by way of wrong estimations at crucial moments and/or questionable decision making. It can be hard to accept one's own failures and/or to admit that a situation or relationship developed differently than expected. If a person loses his partner, child, or other important person in his life, or if a person loses his job, or fails to finish his studies, it can be very difficult to accept the loss or failure. Often people are ashamed to admit their problems, because they fear they will be judged or considered weak. Therefore, people often feel the need to hide their problems from others.

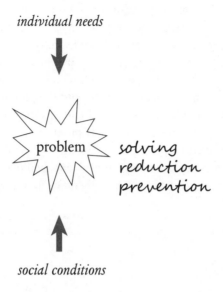

Figure 2.11 Mismatches, problems, and solutions

Because it can be difficult to generate solutions by oneself, quite often people seek the help of a third party. This may be a friend, family member, or neighbour, or possibly a helping professional. In many cases the family doctor is the first professional consulted, then (if people are religious) a pastor, priest or imam, and thirdly, sometimes, a social worker or psychologist.

Asking for help is the crucial first step in the process of changing an individual's situation and finding a solution to one's problems. This is commonly preceded by a painful process and struggle as an individual achieves self-awareness. It is important that volunteer and professional helpers realize that the request for help comes at the end of this difficult process. Itself, recognition of one's need for help is a meaningful step toward finding a solution. To solve, reduce, and prevent further problems, the person seeking help and the actors in his environment need to develop a willingness to see things from a new perspective, behave differently, and cooperate with each other.

I focus here on a goal-oriented process of (behavioural) change that takes place in a specified time-frame, and is meant to change the present adverse circumstances into a desired situation in the end.

However, not all people in distress come to the realization that they need help, or do not always choose to ask for help, and sometimes may not be in the right time or place in their lives to get help. This may be especially true for people seeking to escape or those who remain oblivious of their problems through alcohol, drugs, or other addictions. There are also people who descend into psychoses, people who cut themselves off from the world, and people who may even desire to end their lives just to escape the pain they feel and the problems they face.

Helping professionals are confronted with a variety of people in all sorts of situations and in differen states of mind.

They are expected to act according to their professional standards, and to have the necessary knowledge, means, and facilities to competently assist their clients and patients. Most of them do, and do well.

3.

Development and Change

As people grow and develop, they are in continuous interaction with their environment. If an individual's personal development stagnates and he ends up in undesirable circumstances, the need for change or improvement in his situation arises.

A task of social work is to support individuals, groups, and communities that are in need of such change or improvement. For this reason, the concepts of *development*, *change*, and *improvement* are key words in social work. The phenomenon of *change* in particular is a central concept. In fact, social workers are sometimes referred to as *change agents* (IFSW 2000, p.1).

In this chapter I will discuss the concepts of development, change, and improvement and their relation to one another (Section 3.1), followed by a detailed, didactically constructed overview of various aspects of the central concept of change (Section 3.2). After a historical overview of the theory of planned change (Section 3.3), I give a systematic explanation of a social worker's professional actions, in the form of interventions, aimed at creating change (Section 3.4.1 to 3.4.3). In Section 3.4.4 I place the interventions within the wider methodical and strategic framework to which they belong. I end this chapter with an integrative approach of *social interventions* and forms of *self-control* and *self-steering* based on current theoretical models in social work and connected with the international definition of social work (Section 3.4.5).

3.1 About developing, changing, and improving

The word 'change' has many definitions. In social work, change is perceived as the transformation process from one situation or condition to another. From a time perspective, the existing situation here and now (the situation that has to be changed) is called the starting point, while

77

the situation that social workers attempt to create with and for client(s) (the desired situation) is called the end point. Movement from a starting point to an end point occurs over time, through a transition process or change process.

Change can occur spontaneously, or can be the outcome of a transition process, carefully planned and implemented. A *spontaneous change* is the result of unorganized, random actions and circumstances which mutually influence one another. A *planned change* is the result of goal-oriented, deliberate actions and influenced conditions.

A changed situation or changed conditions can be experienced as an improvement, as a decline, or as neutral, depending on who is affected or confronted with the change. The perception may differ between persons, groups, organizations, or communities. In the case of spontaneous change, it is sometimes questionable who, and to what extent, is better or worse off, and who remains unaffected. In the case of planned change, one tries to create end circumstances that improve the situation or position respective to the previous starting situation. If the desired situation is actually achieved (change processes can fail or not, or work out differently from planned) the 'changer' will experience an improvement in the previous position, situation, or conditions. The question remains as to how the changed situation affects other persons involved, as their experiences may be very different from the 'changer's' experience. This may result in change-oriented action from the other people affected. This reaction is a potential threat to the newly realized situation of the 'changer', and may result in a reversal of the original change.

The opposite of change is continuance: leaving the situation as it is. The latter is not necessarily 'conservative' or 'negative'; neither is striving for change, by definition, always 'progressive' or 'good'.

Change and continuance are relative concepts that can be undone or reversed. Continuance provides security, and a steady, predictable pattern, but change may become necessary to preserve important goods or maintain/uphold values. Nothing remains stagnant; rather, the entire world and the whole universe are in a constant state of evolving and developing.

Humans cannot function without either constancy or change, therefore both change and continuance exist on all levels. Change is challenging and necessary at times, but can also result in unrest and uncertainty. Without change, things may become boring and predictable. However, maintaining constancy may provide stability, security, and respite. As opposites, change and continuance result in tension and dynamics which are preconditions for the need for further development and change.

In planned action toward continuance and change, Zwart and Middel (2005) distinguish different types of interventions, in order of increasing intensity and impact. Figure 3.1 demonstrates this.

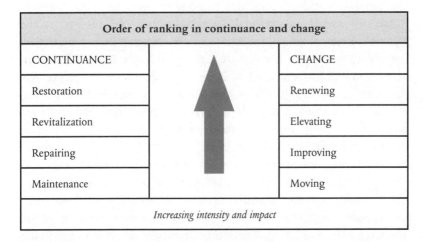

Order of ranking in continuance and change		
CONTINUANCE		CHANGE
Restoration		Renewing
Revitalization		Elevating
Repairing		Improving
Maintenance		Moving
Increasing intensity and impact		

Figure 3.1 Order of ranking in continuance and change
(based on Zwart and Middel 2005, p.60)

In a development process focused on continuance (see left-hand column), the following types of intervention can be used: maintenance (routine maintenance of the existing situation), repairing (restoring to original functioning), revitalization (utilizing an already existing function), and restoration (reconstructing to the original state or function). Maintenance is the least drastic form of continuance; restoration is the most extreme form.

In a development process toward change (see right-hand column), the following interventions can be used: moving (simple rearrangement of elements), improving (accentuating a function and increasing its effectiveness), elevating (qualitative refinement), and renewing (redesigning, reinventing). Moving is the least drastic type of change; renewing is the most extreme type (Zwart and Middel 2005).

In whatever form or nature, change often evokes resistance because it affects the existing situation and the sense of security connected with it. 'Knowing where things stand' often provides more assurance and security than promises for the future or 'wait and see where things stand'. A reserved attitude toward change is understandable and even justifiable in many situations, but is not always the best approach. In some situations change may even be necessary to protect and secure the existing situation against other people's efforts to change it.

From a historical point of view, the 21st century is a hectic time with ongoing change in many aspects of life. Rapid technological changes and worldwide capitalist exploitation generate unprecedented turbulence and dynamics, making people busy and restless, at the expense of relaxation and reflection. Knowledge and beliefs are shaken and the inconceivable becomes reality on all levels and in all sectors. The worldwide financial crisis of 2008 is an example of this: respectable banks and financial institutions went bankrupt, governments of leading capitalist countries nationalized private companies and pumped inconceivably large amounts of money into the economy to prevent an even more devastating economic crisis.

The saying 'not all change is necessarily an improvement' rings true. Change without a well-thought-out purpose or meaning, or change not carefully and meticulously planned and implemented, is often unsuccessful. Such changes frequently cause misunderstanding, chaos, and stagnation, and are a waste of time, money, and resources that could have been used for more constructive purposes.

Change is inevitable. Society is constantly moving and changing because of the ongoing development and mutual influencing of technology, economy, knowledge, religion, and values. No one can escape change, therefore every individual must eventually learn to deal with it. People do so in many different ways.

Figure 3.2 demonstrates change processes in society and how they can be perceived.

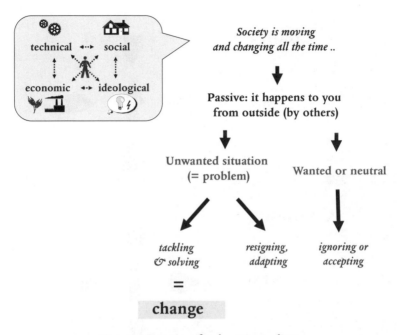

Figure 3.2 Reception of and reaction to change

If changes are unwanted and problematic, people will protest and resist the changes. However, if the effort to resist is too great or seems futile, people will resign themselves to accepting and adapting to the new situation. Similarly, if people are likely to benefit from the changes, they will generally accept them. Lastly, if people remain unaffected by the changes, it is easy to simply ignore them.

The more that people are affected by change in their everyday (micro) environment, the more pressure they will feel to protest and actively resist the change.

People can experience change as something caused externally by others. In other words: as an occurrence, a *change*, that overtakes them and regards them as a passive subject. The first circle in Figure 3.3 demonstrates this.

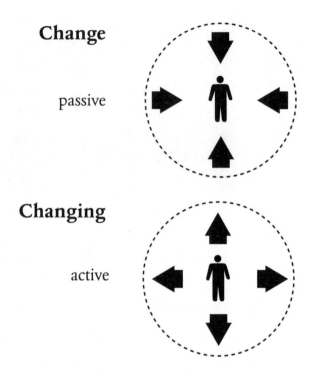

Figure 3.3 Change and changing

If people are faced with change caused by others, they may choose to resist the change and actively seek to stop or undo it (see second circle) while expressing their dissatisfaction. To stop unwanted changes, people have to target the individuals, groups, and organizations that are responsible for causing the changes. To empower themselves, these people have to involve other actors who are in a position to support them and to influence their opponents. In doing this, people are motivated by internal factors, focused on changing the unwanted situation resulting from the actions of others.

3.2 Aspects of change

To outline the most important aspects of change, I have created and use a memory aid (a mnemonic) by forming a word composed by using the first letters of each of the components of *change*.

The word I use is SCANETICS. It does not actually exist in the English language, but is a combination of the existing words SCAN and ETICS. The word 'etics' is from 'etic account', meaning 'a description of a behaviour or belief by an observer, in terms that can be applied to other cultures; that is, an etic account attempts to be "culturally neutral'" (Wikipedia 2011). SCANETICS represents the nine aspects of *change* shown in Figure 3.4.

Scale
Cause
Angle
Nature
Extent
Tempo
Impact
Course
Steering

Figure 3.4 SCANETICS as a memory aid for aspects of change

3.2.1 Scale

Changes occur on one or more scales or levels: micro, meso, or macro. Changes can be restricted to an individual person and his direct surroundings. However, they can extend from the micro level and affect variables on the other scales as well. Interaction between actors on all scales is continuous (see Figure 3.5).

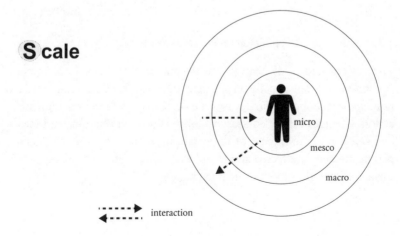

Figure 3.5 Scale of change

Changes on the macro or meso scale such as a government policy or a policy of an important institution (e.g. a hospital, school, or company) generally only have consequences for individual citizens and their direct surroundings. This is also an issue of *power*, whereby a city councillor or the manager of an institution is in charge of the entire municipality or institution which citizens depend on. However, citizens can organize themselves and take action and attempt to force or influence those in authority to change their policy.

3.2.2 Cause

There can be many different reasons to take action in order to effect change, whether as an individual or together with others. One can distinguish between external developments and stimuli, and those coming from within a person or a group.

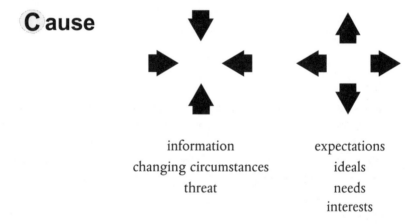

information
changing circumstances
threat

expectations
ideals
needs
interests

Figure 3.6 Cause of change

The various causes of change can be put in order based on urgency. An individual can usually take some time to think over and discuss *new information,* but a *threatening event or development* requires immediate action. Changes can be contrary to long-valued expectations and ideals, and can hamper fulfilment of important needs or desires. In such cases, people are deeply affected and therefore highly motivated to take action toward eliminating the unwelcome changes.

3.2.3 Angle

The impact and significance of a change depends on the scale and position (the point of reference) from which an individual views it.

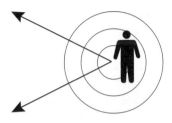

Position, scale and view
from which changes are
measured and judged

Figure 3.7 Angle of change

In general, problems are caused by change processes on the micro, meso, and/or macro scale. Whether, and to what extent, a problem can be characterized as an *individual problem* or as a *social problem* depends on specific aspects of the situation or outcome resulting from the problem.

The effects of losing a loved one, becoming ill, or failing an exam are usually restricted to an individual and his close friends, neighbours, colleagues, and family. These are termed *individual problems*, caused by changes in one's personal sphere.

It is not uncommon for someone to face hardship because of job loss due to reorganization, downsizing, policy change, or cutbacks within a company, institution, or government agency. The individual's problem would therefore be a direct consequence of a larger *social change*. Other persons in a comparable situation would face similar individual consequences due to such social changes.

The viewpoint of the company, institution, or government is that, in order to remain effective, sometimes policy changes or cutbacks may be implemented even if these negatively impact some individuals. Because of this point of view, individual complaints will be treated as *individual problems*, and therefore will be settled independently.

Just as seeing a couple of swallows does not necessarily mean it is summer, the sum of individual problems does not automatically make a *social problem*, despite having the same root causes and similar consequences. The first step is to recognize similar problems and determine the cause(s). If this is realized, the individual problems are more likely to be expressed as a wider social problem that can then be addressed by a group of individuals. If affected individuals unite, they can act jointly to protest against changes, thereby having greater power to stop or fix the *social problem*.

According to the Dutch sociologists Nelissen and de Wit (1991), a *social problem* exists 'if an influential group is of opinion that it is affected by a social situation, that is conflicting with or threatening its values, and that this situation can be improved or changed by collective action' (p.24). Therefore, individuals must unite and together take action to bring the problem under (public) scrutiny, in order for it to be recognized and solved.

This can be a lengthy and difficult struggle. Notably, though, much of the progress in our civilization has occurred because of people who united and fought to liberate themselves and their children and grandchildren from oppression, poverty, discrimination, and degradation. As long as individuals continue to come together and form united fronts, social change and progress will continue.

3.2.4 Nature

Changes can vary in nature. Throughout history, technology, economic activity, knowledge, religion and beliefs, and social developments have been the major *forces of change*. Today, technical, social, economic, and ideological changes continue to influence and interact with each other, creating an endless chain of effects resulting in ongoing change and developments.

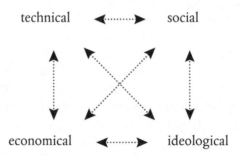

Figure 3.8 Nature of change

A well-known example of a major historical change is the Industrial Revolution of the 19th and 20th centuries. More recent is the electronic revolution, with many economic, social, and ideological effects leading to a new era of information, communication, transportation, and lifestyles.

In many ways, these macro developments (initiated by micro and meso level inventors, researchers, and pioneers) affect people's thoughts and actions, and infiltrate all levels of society in everyday life.

3.2.5 Extent

From a societal perspective, the extent of a change is measured by the number of people affected by it and whether the impact is big or small. However, 'small' and 'big' are relative qualifications. Thus, the changes are qualified depending on the scale, position, and view.

Figure 3.9 Extent of change

A relatively small change on a macro level can have far-reaching consequences on the daily life circumstances of many people. Imagine, for example, a power interruption on a Saturday in a busy shopping district, or in a business centre during the week. On the other hand, a substantial change in an individual's life may have little or no effect on the organizations or institutions which the individual is a member of on the meso and macro levels.

A change experienced by one person as a minor inconvenience may be experienced as a severe problem by another person. This depends on an individual's situation, such as the roles he plays, the resources available to him, and the abilities, attitude, and skills he possesses and utilizes. To fully understand the impact of certain changes on another person or group of persons, it is necessary to have sufficient empathy, and be able to put oneself in the other's position (see also under 'Angle').

3.2.6 Tempo

Change always takes place within a certain time-frame. A change can last a short time or may be long in duration, depending on its qualities and impact. 'Short' and 'long' are relative concepts. As a rule of thumb, short or long lasting time-frames can be measured based on the average lifetime of a human being.

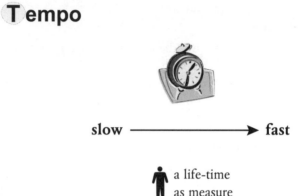

Figure 3.10 Tempo of change

The rate at which a change process occurs is relative, depending on the characteristics and the specific variables existing within the situation. For example, if an individual has to consult a medical specialist for diagnosis or treatment, he may be willing to wait for an hour or two to see the specialist. If surgery is required and there is no urgency, a person may consider a waiting time of three or more months to be acceptable. If an individual drives an old car, he is likely to be willing to have the vehicle inspected once a year. To be educated as a social worker, an education programme with a duration of three or four years is expected. To solve the world hunger crisis, people are prepared to wait another ten years before any major results are seen. A child is given at least 18 years to mature into adulthood. And lastly, to pay off a mortgage, a period of 30 years is generally acceptable.

3.2.7 Impact

A change may be a once in a lifetime occurrence in a relatively short period of time, with a limited impact. However, a change can be of a longer duration, occurring in specific patterns, and having far-reaching, structural, and extensive long-term effects.

Often the government offers limited relief to people on welfare or benefit, or people receiving minimum wages through a non-recurring allowance or a one-time compensation for the rising cost of living. This is a typical example of an *incidental change* with a limited effect on the short-term.

Closing down the coal mines in the UK in the 1980s is an example of a *structural change* with durable, drastic consequences over the long-term. This was the case for the miners and other workers depending on the mines, as well as for the regions where the mines were located. However, this also had lasting structural effects on the whole of society. On a large scale, the switch was made from using coal to other fossilized fuels (oil and natural gas), to nuclear energy, and to clean forms of energy from sunlight, wind, and water.

One can also illustrate this with examples on the micro and meso scale: if someone in his 30s takes a year of unpaid leave from work to travel the world, it is an *incidental change* in the eyes of his colleagues and managers, compared with a 60-year-old who stops working to take early retirement, which is *structural change*.

Having a one-time, short-term sickness, versus having a chronic disease, can be vastly different experiences for affected individuals and their families. A chronic disease is likely to result in many structural consequences for work, housing, mobility, and income, whereas a short-term illness would have little effect on life structures or systems.

I mpact

incidental	$\longrightarrow$	structural
single		drastic
short term		durable

Figure 3.11 Impact of change

3.2.8 Course

The course of a change process can vary; it may be gradual and almost unnoticeable over a long period of time. This type of change process is termed *evolutionary*. However, change can also be very evident, occur quickly and unexpectedly, and have a shocking impact, all over a relatively short time-period. This type of change process is called *revolutionary* change.

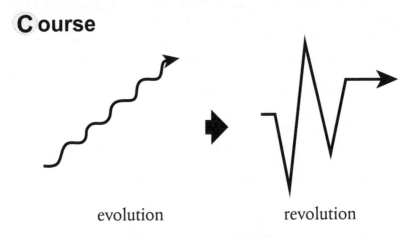

Figure 3.12 Course of change

The evolution of man is an example of a gradual development process over a very long period of time. The worldwide financial crisis of 2008 and the popular uprising against authoritarian regimes in Arab countries in 2011 are examples of revolutionary changes; they occurred unexpectedly, very quickly, and caused many effects with a huge impact in a relatively short time-frame.

3.2.9 Steering

Everything that grows, blossoms, and moves, including mother earth, is continuously developing. Life is like an unremitting movie reel, not like a photo or snapshot that only captures a single moment in time. However, the movie called 'reality' has not one director but many directors who, mostly without consultation or coordination, edit portions of the *film of life* according to their own views, goals, and interests.

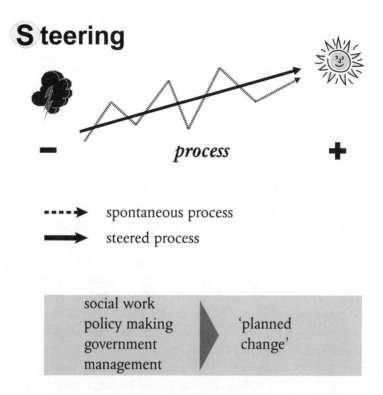

Figure 3.13 Steering of change

Persons, groups, organizations, and communities are always busy creating change, by initiating and stimulating developments toward a (future) situation that is in their own best interest, and improves their position and situation. To do this successfully, each of these actors gathers knowledge and resources, works according to a plan, and encourages cooperation between other involved actors.

If an actor understands the development processes in which other actors are involved, that actor increases his ability to steer the process in the direction he chooses. This is *planned change*: steering development processes in a desired direction.

Planning of change and steering of processes are key activities for many professionals, institutions, companies, and governments. Managers of these organizations are constantly busy influencing and steering internal and external processes through implementation of rules and policies, as well as resource management. Similarly, teachers, doctors, nurses, researchers, social workers, and engineers influence and steer various processes within their respective professional fields. Teachers stimulate and encourage the development of skills, abilities, and professional competency of their students. Doctors and nurses attempt to diagnose numerous illnesses, diseases, and handicaps of their patients, and treat them throughout the duration of the healing process. Social workers empower and support their clients to better understand their own situation in order to change it and move toward a more satisfying, better quality of life.

3.3 Planned change and beyond

Planning of change is a common job expectation for organizational consultants, policy makers, teachers, and helping professionals, including social workers.

Research and theory development on the subject of change began in the United States after World War II. In the uncompromising social climate of the Cold War between East and West, interest in this subject gained momentum in an (ideological) movement that tried to exceed the rigid planning practice of Communism and the indifferent, blind market mechanism of Capitalism. The guiding principle behind this is that of the responsible, rational man, taking his future into his own hands, and realizing his ambitions in a carefully planned manner, with the help of scientific-based methods (Cozijnsen and Vrakking 2003).

The wider scientific-based interest for change includes planned change, organization development, and management theory, with planned change having the longest history. Planned change is also known as: 'Theory of Change', 'Planning of Change', and 'Dynamics of Change'. Well-known publications are *Field Theory and Social Research* by Kurt Lewin (1951), *The Dynamics of Planned Change* by Lippitt, Watson, and Westley (1958), *The Planning of Change* by Bennis *et al.* (1969), and *Strategies for Planned Change* by Zaltman and Duncan (1977) (Cozijnsen and Vrakking 2003, p.22).

Because of planned change, the focus shifted from a change of ideology to technocratic (i.e. instrumental) forms of change. This resulted in an approach in which experts developed plans that may or may not be improved by people involved in it. In 1958, Lippitt *et al.* described planned change 'as an outcome of a conscious decision to realize improvements in an individual system, achieved with help of professional support' (Cozijnsen and Vrakking 2003, p.22). In the changing social climate after 1960, this autocratic view was replaced by a clinical approach to change that remains fundamental today for many methodical approaches. In a clinical approach, helping professionals always work in dialogue, meeting with their customers or clients to realize changes. In 1974, Bennis *et al.* described planned change as 'a process of conscious change that makes use of valid knowledge, and is based on the right culture and cooperation between the "change agent" and the "client system"' (Cozijnsen and Vrakking 2003, p.22).

Kurt Lewin is another social scientist commonly linked to, and strongly identified with, planned change. Besides making an important contribution to group dynamics and action research, Lewin describes in *Field Theory and Social Research* (1951) the behaviour of individuals, groups and organizations as the outcome of a dynamic balance of opposite forces. Driving forces facilitate change, because they steer individuals, groups, and organizations in the desired direction ('pull'), while restraining forces slow down that change and have opposite effects ('push'). To allow for change to be possible, one has to analyse the active forces, surrender the existing balance, and create a new situation of balance.

According to Lewin, this can be done by means of a three-step process, consisting of the successive phases of unfreezing, moving, and (re)freezing (Figure 3.14).

unfreezing ➡ moving ➡ (re)freezing

Figure 3.14 Three-step process, based on Lewin (1951)

Unfreezing (defrosting, releasing) is the phase in which the quasi-balance is temporarily switched off; steady reaction patterns are released and new behaviour is stimulated. The goal of this phase is to weaken the forces (habits, standards, and values) of the target system (the client) that were causing or exacerbating the client's problems and preventing solutions. Clients have to be motivated to change and be conscious of the need for change. Correspondingly, the helping professional must be open-minded and non-judgemental in order to earn the trust of the client, and support the client in his efforts.

Moving (action toward a better, future situation) means that the target system moves to a new level of balance by developing new behaviour and standards, as well as an appropriate attitude. The helping professional encourages the client by supporting changes in the direct environment (structure, work processes, behavioural rules, etc.) and by giving him tasks to aid in achieving positive change.

(Re)freezing (consolidating/securing change) is aimed at strengthening and internalizing (making it one's own) new, effective patterns of behaviour. This step involves establishing and anchoring the newly developed situation, and maintaining the new balance between forces. This is done with the help of structural and cultural changes that support the newly realized situation. Examples are: making agreements and acting according to them, applying new standards, implementing new policies, and practising the new way of organizing.

Lippitt *et al.* (1958) extended Lewin's theory to a process involving seven stages. They focus on tasks and activities of the 'change agent', not on the development of the change process as such. The seven steps of Lippitt *et al.* (1958) are as follows:

1. Diagnose the problem. Make use of key persons for gathering information and solving problems.

2. Assess the current motivation and capacity for change.

3. Assess the motivation and resources of the change agent. This includes the change agent's involvement, commitment to change, available resources, ambitions, and position.

4. Select appealing dynamic change objects. Develop an action plan, appropriate strategies, and criteria for evaluation.

5. Agree on the role of the change agent. His role(s) should be understood by all actors involved, so that expectations are clear. Roles of the change agent can be cheerleader, expert, consultant, and/or facilitator.

6. Consolidate changes. Communication, feedback, and coordination are essential elements in this stage.

7. Pay attention to the helping relationship. The change agent should transfer his roles and gradually withdraw. This will occur when the change becomes part of everyday life and functioning of the client system.

Phase models in Planned Change Theory, like those of Lewin and Lippitt *et al.* are based on underlying strategies with different assumptions of human behaviour.

Bennis *et al.* (1985) also studied change strategies. They distinguish between three different kinds:

- *Rational-empirical strategies.* These occur when people are rational and follow their self-interest, once it is revealed to them. Change is based on information, communication, and expected profits.

- *Normative-re-educative strategies.* These are meant to stimulate and motivate people to realize change through self-generated ideas for improvement. This is a bottom-up approach in which people are active, social beings, willing to learn and act according to standards and values. Change is the outcome of redefining and reinterpreting existing standards and values, based on sufficient public support.

- *Power-coercive strategies.* These are used to force changes from a position of power. This is a top-down approach in which people are basically compliant and will generally do what they are told or made to do. Power and authority are necessary to realize desired behaviour in power-coercive strategies.

Although it is possible to be confronted with each of these strategies in its purest form, in general a mix of them will be used in a planned change process.

Figure 3.15 shows the three strategies of Bennis *et al.*, each surrounded by their characteristics.

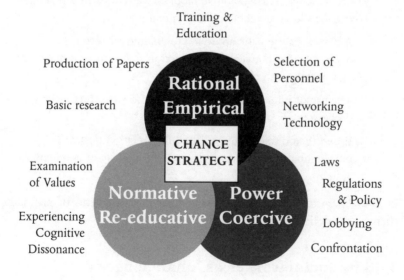

Figure 3.15 Strategies of change, surrounded by their characteristics (based on Bennis et al. 1985)

Since 1950, Planned Change theories have impacted social workers and professionals from various other fields who deal with change processes. According to Cozijnsen and Vrakking (2003), 'the scientific knowledge of change processes is maximally utilized to give action of helping professionals a rational character' (pp.22–23, translation WB). Encouraged and supported by policy makers, behavioral scientists bridged the division between science and practice by implementing science in practice. Planned Change Theory has undoubtedly become an applied science.

Its application in various fields of society has resulted in a variety of applied sciences and theories.

Some of the field-oriented change theories, such as organization theory and organization development, are world renowned. Planned Change concepts and theories have also been integrated into management theory, business administration, public administration, science of policy/political science, nursing skills and social work theories and methodologies such as advanced forms of social case work, group work, community development, family therapy, and social intervention. While these applied and modified variations of Planned Change are being utilized in various fields, there are still scientists and researchers working on the general (meta) level of Planned Change Theory or Development Theory.

Planned Change Theory and its applied variations in all different fields have the following characteristics in common:

- A planned systematic approach to change processes, distinguishing between various action stages such as diagnosis, goal setting, and choice of strategy.

- The use of interventions to influence and steer/guide change processes.

- Entering and maintaining a (helping) relation between professional worker (as service system) and client (as client system).

In the next section, I will demonstrate how these elements of planned change are applied in social work.

3.4 The social worker as 'change agent'

Because the phenomenon of *change* is a central concept in social work, in this section I discuss how and why social workers apply concepts and theories of planned *change* in their work. I conclude with some new ideas and concepts characterized by integration and holism.

3.4.1 Spontaneous and planned change

If a person, group, organization, or community is experiencing problems, is dissatisfied with current positions and conditions, or is seeking further development, those affected can take action to change the situation into a more desirable state.

Awareness of one's own situation and the decision to change it are the first steps in the development process that lead to a new situation. The aim is for the new circumstance to be a comparable improvement over the situation that existed before the change process began.

This process can be pictured as shown in Figure 3.16.

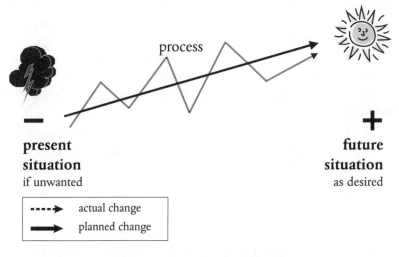

present situation
if unwanted

future situation
as desired

----▶ actual change
——▶ planned change

Figure 3.16 Planned and actual change

Because the development process leads to a better future situation than the present one and is intended to achieve a transformation, it can be characterized as a *change process*.

If the change process is successful, the new, more desirable situation will be on a higher level in terms of Maslow's Hierarchy of Needs (see Section 2.2.1). In spiritual terms, the realization of betterment can be described as a step from the darkness into the light. In Figure 3.16, the dark clouds over the present situation and a bright sun above the desired, future situation symbolize this.

Because nature, human life, and society are all continuously developing, growing, and changing, one's current situation is like a snapshot from an ongoing film, as a result or outcome of the ongoing 'spontaneous' and steered change process from a previous time. If people want to improve their own circumstances, they make choices that influence or direct an ongoing, existing development into a desired direction.

To move from an existing situation toward a desired future situation, it is necessary to analyse and understand current and ongoing developments in order to influence them and guide them in the desired direction.

This taps into the core of Planned Change Theory: the planning and steering of change processes. To move from an existing situation to a desired situation, one has to initiate, stimulate, and support a structured, goal-oriented change process. This transformation process includes many aspects, occurring on various levels within a specific, meaningful social-cultural context.

On a conceptual level, change is a matter of moving from one situation or state to another. The process of change is influenced by setting and achieving three types of goals: transformation, reduction, and application:

- *Transformation goals* are aimed at assessment and identification of the different stages between the original situation and the end situation.

- *Reduction goals* are intended to create optimum conditions and to implement workable means to achieve the objectives of the change process.

- *Application goals* intend to mobilize people and means, and to generate the time that is necessary to realize the desired situation.

Planned change is a demanding exercise. Many questions concerning 'how', 'what', and 'why' regarding the desired change need to be answered in an effective, satisfying way, while the process itself requires hard work to maintain it and to achieve the intended results.

3.4.2 Problem-solving models

A planned, steered change process is goal-oriented, develops in stages, and is based on a plan or programme made beforehand, through dialogue and agreement with client, patient, or customer.

In planned change theories within social work and other change oriented professions, many of these problem-solving models, or change models, are circulating. All organization, treatment, and consultation theories as well as methods, programmes, and therapies, work with their own change model. These models can be visualized in the form of a stairway, a wheel, a cycle, or cylinder to assist in memorizing the stages of the change process and simplify its application.

All of the change models are based on an elementary problem-solving model. A problem-solving model contains answers to successive basic questions such as *what* (diagnosis), *why* (objective), and *how* (process), after which the answers are applied in practice (carrying out) and the end situation is compared with the start situation (evaluation).

The Stairway of Change

Drawing 2 demonstrates the basic change model using the 'Stairway of Change' as an analogy.

Social workers initiate and support change processes aimed at improving the situation of the client in comparison to his existing situation where he may be experiencing hopelessness, depression, negativity, or limited options. The desired situation exists on a higher level, offering the client hope and a greater chance of happiness and success in life.

If a person, group, organization, or community makes a request for a social worker's assistance, it is because one has become aware of the negative effects of his own state or situation, and realizes the possible consequences to his own needs, interests, position, and perspectives.

During the first meeting (the intake) with the client, the social worker starts *gathering information* about the problem, as well as about the process of awareness and motivation that led to the client's request for help. If the client and social worker decide to cooperate, thereby taking on the roles of 'client' and 'helper', they continue discussing relevant information about the problem, any significant history or background, and the client's social surroundings. The social worker explores the needs and desires of the client(s), possibilities for change, support and cooperation from others, and the assistance available from the social worker and his institution.

Drawing 2 The Stairway of Change (© Henny Feijer)

If sufficient information is gathered, the social worker and the client conduct an *analysis* of the client's existing situation, evaluating the influence of other people and circumstances, the client's role, and the client's own assessment of the situation.

In the next stage of *problem formulation*, the client and social worker come to an agreement on the concrete problems that will be targeted and the order in which the client and social worker will address the issues.

By involving the client in the assessment of his situation and discussing possibilities for change, means of the client, and support available from others including the social worker and other professionals, it is possible to *set a goal* that can realistically be achieved.

Means in various forms (such as money, facilities, expertise, time, and abilities) are important for facilitating the client's ability to take action. If means are insufficient, they may need to be supplemented, or assistance may be required to secure alternative resources.

Based on available information, analysis of the situation, problem formulation, goal setting, and means, the social worker and client have to agree on a *strategy*. In order for a strategy to be realistic and feasible, it should incorporate the client's ideas, goals, abilities, and desire for change as well as the means of attaining his goal. The strategy should also be based on an estimation of cooperation and support from others, as well as a risk analysis and expected challenges and barriers throughout the process.

In the *programming* stage, the social worker and the client make a plan or programme, whereby it is determined in what way, with what means, involving whom, and at what time certain actions will be taken and/or activities executed to achieve the pre-established goal. This is done in stages and within a scheduled time-frame (planning). Programming must be carefully planned, and if appropriate should involve others. It is also important for social worker and client to agree on the plan of action, and to communicate clearly and in a straightforward manner.

Carrying out the programme requires the investment of time, means, energy, and attention. The client should report progress, stagnation, successes, and obstacles and discuss these with the social worker. If necessary, the original programme may need to be adjusted or revised to improve the client's chances of succeeding.

Evaluation occurs through the change process, as well as at its conclusion. Throughout the process, progress is compared with the planning, and the actual end situation is measured next to the desired situation. Successes and failures are discussed, conclusions are made, the programme is revised, and the planning restructured based on the evaluations.

Social workers can make use of a variety of change models to structure their professional actions. I focus here on two, the so-called

'Eight Steps Model of Reintegration in Society' (used in the Netherlands for homeless clients receiving care, and in the Ukraine for women in social adaptation work) (Leeuwen-den Dekker *et al.* 2006), and the 'Cycle of Change' of Prochaska and DiClemente (1982), used to help clients with addiction issues.

The Eight Steps Model

The intent of the Eight Steps Model of Reintegration in Society is to aid social workers and their clients in reaching targets by working together in a structured manner. This improves clients' ability to help themselves and to attain the best possible way of life. 'An important feature of the work…is that each client has a case manager (the other term used is 'a curator') who provides individual support for the client. Each social worker assists several clients' (Leeuwen-den Dekker *et al.* 2006, p.11).

The Eight Steps Model focuses on working with positive characteristics and strengths that are already present in the life of every individual. This includes status, finances, residence, social behaviour, mental condition, physical condition, employment, motivation, practical skills, and involvement in various activities.

The model structures activities of both client and case manager, and helps to define goal-oriented actions and tools to use in the planned activities.

The benefits of using the model are (p.12):

- It provides a more complete picture of a client.
- It guides the work from start to finish.
- It helps social workers to express and assess professional and personal capacity.
- It stimulates teamwork, with all its positive effects.

The Eight Steps Model divides the individual path of homeless clients in care in the Netherlands into eight stages, each with its own specific targets, methods, and instruments. The Ukrainian workers adjusted the model, in particular by renaming the first three steps.

Figure 3.17 shows both the Dutch and Ukrainian versions of the Eight Steps Model.

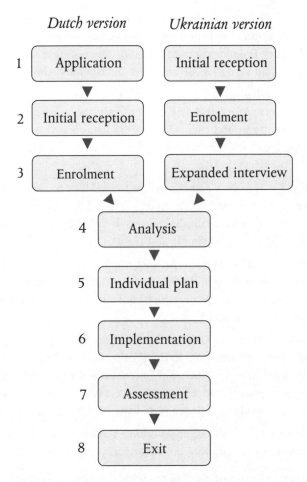

*Figure 3.17 The Eight Steps Model of Reintegration in Society
(based on Leeuwen-den Dekker et al. 2006)*

- *Step 1 – Application.* This is the first contact between client and/or his representative and institution. 'Several standard questions (e.g. client's age, whether having children, what basic problems) should be clarified' (p.14).

- *Step 2 – Initial reception.* An initial interview is conducted to find out whether there is a match between client and institution. Issues are: reasons for applying, personal history, major problems, expected assistance, and information on services provided by the institution.

- *Step 3 – Enrolment.* This includes: preparing a room, showing client around the institution, introduction to other clients, and allowing time for client to settle in. There should be a list of enrolment activities for both case manager and the client.

- *Step 4 – Analysis.* All components of well-being are discussed in the course of regular meetings (at least once a week) between case manager and client. Each component is discussed and reported 'with the focus on a client's strengths and not just on the problems' (p.14).

- *Step 5 – Individual plan.* Based on the analysis in step 4, case manager and client make an individual support plan for the upcoming several months. The goals formulated in this plan should be specific, simple and realistic.

- *Step 6 – Implementation.* This step implies 'actions aimed at resolving priority problems described in the action plan, establishment of the necessary contacts, and restoration of essential skills' (p.15).

- *Step 7 – Assessment.* Joint review by client and case manager of what has been done in the previous phase. Based on the results, a new description of functions and a new individual support plan is made. 'Thus, the cycle is repeated again and again till a client feels ready to leave an institution' (p.15).

- *Step 8 – Exit.* This last stage is aimed at preparing the client for leaving the institution, both physically and emotionally.

Like all other change models, this model is theoretical. It ideally serves as a tool and guideline. In reality, various stages overlap each other, or transitions can be more abrupt than expected. A planned change process can be disrupted in many different ways: for example, if there is more opposition and less cooperation than anticipated; or if a client loses hope and wants to give up. If the change process lasts longer than expected the social worker may run out of time and may not be granted any more time from the institution he works for. Generally, no matter how carefully constructed, the original planning usually needs to be revised during its implementation.

The Cycle of Change Model

As demonstrated, the course of a change process can be represented in the form of successive steps or stages, like a stairway. Another effective visual aid is that of a cycle, or even better: a spiral (Figure 3.18).

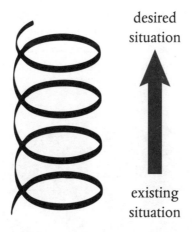

desired
situation

existing
situation

Figure 3.18 Spiral of change

For at least three reasons, the spiral is an appropriate analogy of a change process:

1. Like a stairway (see Figure 3.22), a spiral can go up or down, but in a more fluent, cyclical motion. One spiral represents a step in the change process. In my opinion the spiral is a more direct reflection of the reality of change than a step, because it offers endless possibilities for moving up or down.

2. In a spiral you can fall back (you cannot fall out) or climb your way up. Falling down (letting yourself go) is easier than the hard work of climbing up.

3. The spiral as a metaphor of the course of change is more closely connected with common language: individuals, groups, organizations, and communities can slip into a 'downward spiral' of development or can initiate action and encourage an 'upward spiral' of development.

A well-known, frequently used, spiral model of change is the 'Cycle of Change Model' of Prochaska and DiClemente (1982) who conducted research into addiction and possible methods to kick addictive habits. The model has been applied to cope with a range of addiction issues, such as smoking, alcoholism, drugs, and related problems. The model is aimed at individual behavioural change and is therefore useful in psychotherapy, but can also be utilized effectively in social work.

In accordance with planned change theories, Prochaska and DiClemente consider *change* as a process in time in which many factors and actors play a role. People can move forward or backward in the change process and may even get stuck in certain stages.

The Cycle of Change Model includes six cycles or phases a person encounters on the path of change. The upward motion moves clockwise (Figure 3.19).

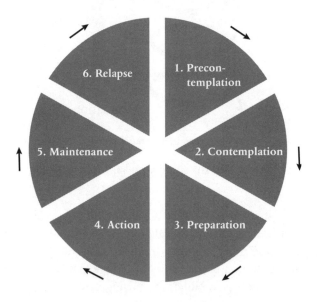

Figure 3.19 The Cycle of Change Model (based on Prochaska and DiClemente 1982)

1. In the phase of *precontemplation*, the client is not yet thinking about changing behaviour, but begins doing so as he moves into the next stage.

2. In the phase of *contemplation*, the client becomes aware of his problematic behaviour, but is ambivalent about what to do. It can be a difficult phase, trying to decide between continuing or changing behaviour.

3. In the *preparation* phase, the client is taking steps towards changing his behaviour. This may be done by reducing the frequency of the problem behaviour or by stopping it altogether.

4. The *action* phase is characterized by efforts to adopt a new set of behaviours. Various activities are undertaken to support the new behaviours and ensure they continue.

5. *Maintenance* is the phase in which the change has been integrated into the client's way of life. Activities are aimed at internalizing and securing the positive behaviours and changes.

6. *Relapse*, or a return to the old behaviour, is always a possibility. It is not inevitable, but does often occur. However, this should not be seen as a failure. People often relapse several times before they succeed in realizing permanent new behaviour. If the client permanently avoids returning to the problem behaviour, this means he can control or manage the problem, but the problem has not actually disappeared. The client might still get cravings to smoke, drink, or take drugs, but as long as he avoids actually doing it, he will avoid its harmful physical effects.

The Cycle of Change Model demonstrates the process of replacing existing problematic habits with new, more constructive behaviours. The stages do not unfold in a linear way, but rather in a cyclic manner. Actual change generally occurs by trial and error, and often by repeating the same steps several times before achieving success.

Clients often fall back into old habits in the action and maintenance phases. Some clients stop the therapy or programme, while others do not give up entirely, but have to start over again in the contemplation phase with a new goal and renewed incentive. Obese individuals and clients with addiction problems often repeat the first cycles before they manage to move into the next. Successful are those who learn from their failures and do not circle endlessly on the same level.

3.4.3 Interventions

To steer processes in a desired direction, client and social worker have to intervene at appropriate moments in these processes. Intervening is the active application of *interventions*. An intervention is defined as a conscious, goal-oriented action to influence the behaviour of individuals, groups, organizations, and communities, as well as the course of events, and to steer them in a specific, desired direction.

Figure 3.20 provides an image of the peaks and valleys of success and failure of interventions throughout the change process.

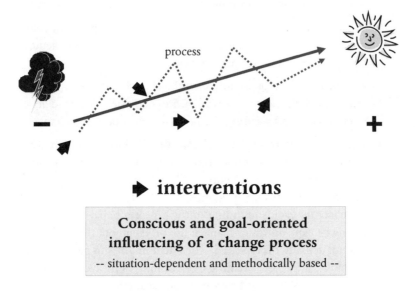

➡ interventions

**Conscious and goal-oriented
influencing of a change process**
-- situation-dependent and methodically based --

Figure 3.20 Interventions in a change process

Interventions in change processes can be through the client, a person, group, organization, or community involved, and/or in a professional manner by the social worker.

Deciding which intervention is appropriate to use depends on each particular situation and its context, as well as the method which the intervention is part of. It is necessary for interventions to be based on defensible arguments and research in order for change efforts to be successful. Content, type, intensity, and duration of time required have to match the subject, client, target group, context, and situation. Interventions should occur at a suitable time and should work within the actual stage of the change process. The means utilized should be effective, while the client also needs support and cooperation of others in order to implement and maintain new behaviours.

There are many different types of intervention, and they vary in intensity or depth. Interventions can be part of a methodology or a policy of a professional team or institution, and are tied to the rules and the ethical code of the helping professional.

Figure 3.21 provides a brief overview of interventions.

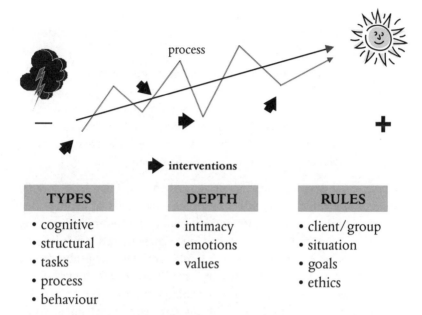

TYPES	**DEPTH**	**RULES**
• cognitive	• intimacy	• client/group
• structural	• emotions	• situation
• tasks	• values	• goals
• process		• ethics
• behaviour		

Figure 3.21 Types and characteristics of social interventions

An intervention is an effort to influence an actual development process, while *steering* can be defined as the application of a series of well-thought-out, goal-oriented interventions in a change process:

- In *cognitive interventions*, knowledge and information are used to influence behaviour, thinking, and underlying visions. Think of books, articles, lecturing, training, instruction, learning tasks, movies, and documentaries.

- *Structural interventions* are goal-oriented methods of constructing and designing buildings, appliances, waiting and consulting rooms, classrooms, meeting places, transit stations, public transport vehicles, etc. They initiate, motivate, and/or guide a desired behaviour or idea into fruition.

- Giving people a specific *task or assignment* in their role as client, patient, worker, or student is another way to influence their behaviour. This occurs by placing them in situations where they are confronted with issues and people with which and with whom they have to cope in order to fulfil the task or assignment.

- *Process interventions* are used to discuss and influence communicative messages through gestures, mimicry, physical contact, and eye contact.

- *Behavioural interventions* are aimed at trying out new behaviour in specific situations. They are direct forms of task interventions. Behavioural interventions can be profound, because problems are often private, sensitive matters, deeply connected to people's emotions. Social workers are expected to operate with integrity and professionalism.

Helping professionals, such as social workers, are bound by specific standards and rules, as described in professional codes of conduct (see Section 1.2 for the social work code of conduct). In everyday practice, the professional code is interpreted and implemented according to specific standards and rules. Two examples are: 'Do not probe deeper into sensitive matters than necessary' and 'Respect the limits of the client'. A general recommendation to helping professionals is to network with colleagues so as to discuss difficult cases and uncertainties, while protecting confidentiality and privacy of clients.

In this chapter, I explained that an intervention is an effort to steer an actual change process. Steering is the application of a series of well-thought-out, goal-oriented interventions in an existing development process. Interventions have various characteristics and can be applied according to a specific pattern. If this is the case, they become part of a specific methodology.

The next section explains this in greater detail.

Figure 3.22 Winding staircase in Ghent (Belgium)

3.4.4 Methods and strategy

To understand change processes in and around the client system, and to channel them in a desired direction, it is necessary to plan a series of well-thought-out, goal-oriented interventions. If these interventions are performed in a systematic way, according to a pattern, they are part of a specific *methodology*.

A methodology is a coherent whole made up of interconnected concepts, instruments, means, and instructions, with the objective being to analyse and solve (psychosocial) problems. The psychosocial nature of the problems targeted by the methodology makes it a *social work methodology*.

A methodology of social work is based on a developmental theory or a strategy of change, or at least on a comprehensive series of notions in that sphere. The lower instrumental levels of a methodology nearly always consist of a mix of actual and new approaches and techniques. Figure 3.23 shows the elements of a methodology in hierarchical order. The arrow on the bottom symbolizes the steering of change processes, where methologies in social work are used for.

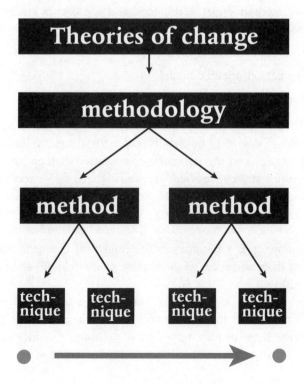

Figure 3.23 Theoretical hierarchy of interventions

If a methodology is an implementation of a specific theoretical change or developmental strategy, it is deemed 'applied scientific knowledge' that works in a *deductive* way, that is from general to specific. If a methodology is the outcome of systematic reflection on practice, it is expressed as 'a generalized experience' which means working in an *inductive* way by deriving general concepts from specific situations.

Besides deductive and inductive reasoning, there is also *adductive* reasoning (finding a suitable explanation for a series of events) and *analogue reasoning* (jumping from one specific situation to another and drawing plausible conclusions).

In the 20th century, social workers and social scientists developed, applied, and published methodologies that have become part of the international body of knowledge of social work (see Section 1.4). Methodologies can be categorized according to specialization (see Chapter 5) and the underlying vision and theory of man, society, development, and change.

Inspired by the three different types of change strategies formulated by Bennis *et al.* (discussed in Section 3.3), the Dutch social work theorist Gerard Donkers described three models (or strategies) of change which social work methodologies, techniques, and approaches are based on. These models of change in social work are:

- the social-technological model
- the person-oriented model
- the society-critical model.

The first two models correspond with two of the three strategies of planned change described by Bennis *et al.* (1985), namely, the rational-empirical strategy and the normative-re-educative strategy (see Section 3.3). The third strategy, power-coercive, is part of Donkers' society-critical model in the tradition of change theories related to Habermas, and is a reflection of the roaring 1960s and the following democratization period.

The following is a summary of the content of Donkers' models of change and their references to social work methodologies and methods (Donkers 2005).

In the *social-technological model*, humans are seen as basic rational beings who are able to regulate their behaviour and adapt to their environment. In a democratic country, upbringing, education, peer groups, and mass media influence people's behaviour toward each other on the various scales of social life. In this model, professional action is based on rational-empirical evidence and scientific knowledge.

The social worker helps clients to change their behaviour and to influence their environment. Although the social worker is the expert, the relationship between worker and client is intended to be mutual; the people involved influence each other. Contact and empathy are crucial elements of the relationship and are important factors for achieving results. Worker and client have a contract and work according to an action plan.

Methods, approaches, and methodologies based on a social-technological model are numerous. For example, problem-oriented methods, behavioural-cognitive methods, social-technical system approach, communication approach, rational-decision methods, task-oriented help, planned-change methods, and group dynamics are some of these theories and models.

The *person-oriented model* is based on a positive view of humankind. Individuals are responsible for themselves and have freedom of choice. Structure and culture are created by people in continuous interaction with their environment. Science is bound to values and standards, fulfils tasks in society, and has co-responsibility for practices in everyday life. Scientists of the humanistic school in social sciences are representatives of this model.

The social worker works in dialogue with his clients. Mutual acceptance is an important condition. The interaction between worker and client is not only a means, but also the objective of the change process. The professional relationship is meant to stimulate personal growth and interpersonal relations. The social worker is expected to be authentic, with non-judgemental, balanced feelings, views, and behaviour.

Characteristic of this model are methods and approaches such as: psychosynthesis, Gestalt, the client-centred approach, modern forms of human relations management, experimental interpersonal therapy, encounter, meditation, Theme-Centred Interaction (TCI), biodynamics, the dialogical model of social activation work (Baart), the locality-approach in community work, and psycho-energetic therapy.

In a *society-critical model*, humans are seen as mutually connected social beings who form one entity with their environment. The economic processes of production, distribution, and consumption strongly influence people's needs, desires, and developments in society.

Facts and findings within the sciences presented as 'objective' are often the outcome of political choices, determined by existing interests and power balances in society. Ideally, scientific work should be objective, but this is not always realistic in practice. From a social-critical point of view, association and connection with the less powerful people in society is needed to stimulate more social justice in society. Power is an important factor for functioning and success within society. Social awareness and dialectic thinking are key in the explanation of human behaviour. The relation between 'being' and 'awareness' is crucial in critical analysis of social developments.

A critical social worker is aware of power differences in his relation with clients. An effective professional relationship is one of mutual learning in which equality and a (power) free dialogue is the goal. The social worker encourages and supports self-regulation and independence of clients. Interventions of clients and social workers aim for personal development, adaptation, and change of cultural and social aspects of the environment.

The society-critical model of change includes the following methods and approaches: methods of critical psychology, critical empowerment approach, exemplary learning, politicizing learning, gender-specific approach, labour rehabilitation, left-radical approach of action and education, management of social inequality, awareness method of Freire, social-ecological approach, emancipating help (Donkers 2005).

Donkers' three models of change cover existing approaches, techniques, and methodologies in social work. Together, they take into account all aspects of social work as described in the international definition of social work: changing, solving problems, developing, strengthening, liberating, enhancing well-being, interaction, influencing, realizing human rights, and stimulating social justice (IFSW 2000; see Chapter 1).

From the viewpoint of professional practitioners, the common elements of the change models seem to be as relevant, or even more relevant, than the differences between them. Moreover, notwithstanding the similarities between the three models, the differences seem to have an added function.

Donkers was the first to recognize this, and he made note of six important similarities between the three change models in social work (Donkers 2005, Chapter 8):

1. The voluntary and dialogical relation between client and social worker.

2. The focus on democratization and humanization of society.

3. Recognition and stimulation of self-regulation and influencing the environment as important aims of professional action.

4. Openness toward a need for empirical research.

5. Recognizing and acknowledging that both harmony and conflict tactics can be part of professional interventions.

6. Awareness of the need for concrete, attainable goals in the short term, and preventive goals in the long term.

The differences between the three models are as notable and instructive as the similarities. From the social-technological model, one can learn that it is not necessary to translate everything in ideological terms, but rather remain open-minded as to the usefulness of social-technological aspects of social work and the appeal of attainable goals.

The person-oriented change model emphasizes the danger of the social-technological model: reducing the client to an object of behavioural change. This model offers an alternative by emphasizing the ability of the individual to choose, to act, and to construct.

The society-critical model demonstrates a broader view of a client's social problems by including the societal, political, and environmental dimensions in professional analysis and interventions.

I fully agree with Donkers. In my opinion, this is not simply a plea for an eclectic approach, but recognition of the need for a more extensive, integrative theory of social work that goes beyond the well laid out instrumental theory of planned change.

Donkers did what he promised in 2005 in the 11th edition (!) of his *Veranderkundige modellen* (*Models of Change*): he performed an empirical and theoretical search for elements to construct a broad, integrative theory of change in social work.

3.4.5 Integrative approach: towards a new methodology of changing

Donkers unfolds his new Integrative Theory of Changing in his book *Grondslagen van veranderen* (*Foundations of changing*), published in 2010. He defines changing as a form of action in which subjects realize certain goals which refer to values of behaviour. The action itself is performed within a process of becoming different, and various self-regulating activities are involved (p.14). Changing is a reflective process of self-steering and adapting, a form of self-regulation (p.99), because it is dependent on person(s) and context, and it is continuously interacting with behaviour, person, and environment.

Donkers provides a 'Three Worlds Scheme of Changing' to illustrate this concept (Figure 3.24).

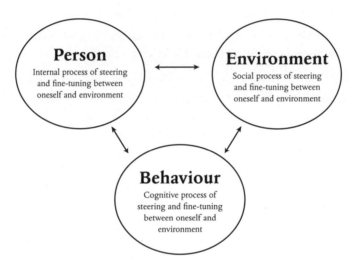

Figure 3.24 Three Worlds Scheme of Changing (Donkers 2010, p.99; approved translation)

The diagram shows the processes of interaction between behaviour, person, and environment. These three elements have mutual influence on each other in every action situation. They represent closely interwoven clusters of factors, but the relative influence of each factor can differ depending on the person and situation.

Each of the three worlds is connected with one of Donkers' three change models in social work discussed and explained in Section 3.4.4.

- The *World of Behaviour* is emphasized in the social-technological change model. Steering and fine-tuning are used to initiate and support particular behavioural reference values in a specific context.

  It concerns the internal and external cognitive quality or adequateness of observations, interpretations, goal selections, expectations, strategic decisions and behaviour. These cognitive aspects of behaviour address a wide arsenal of themes, theories and methodical guidelines... It is essential to connect this cognitive knowledge with ethics. (Donkers 2010, pp.99–100)

- The *World of the Person* is the playground of the person-oriented change model. It concerns intrapersonal regulation of emotions and motivations or an individual's ability to base action on real needs, feelings, and desires. It concerns a multi-dimensional self-concept, based on individual's ability 'to create an inner balance between body, common sense, feelings, intuition, and behaviour in different social roles and situations' (p.100).

This approach is practised in a wide range of theories, methodologies, therapies, and methods. It is important to adapt and combine these approaches and methods with cognitive and society-critical strategies and methodologies.

- In the *World of the Environment*, steering and fine-tuning are aimed at regulating social relations between individuals, groups, organizations, and communities and their social and ecological environments. The critical social change model is a strategy that fits in this World. In the Environmental World, emphasis is placed on the social quality of life on a cultural, interpersonal, and structural level. To avoid bias, it is necessary to adopt and integrate cognitive, ethical, and person-oriented approaches (in Donkers 2010).

Integrated, change-oriented actions from any of these three Worlds require a certain level of knowledge, abilities, and skills, as well as the proper approach, in order to be successful.

For those reasons Donkers presents a reflection model, including a total of nine basic competencies for self-regulation, three for each 'World' theory, in Figure 3.25.

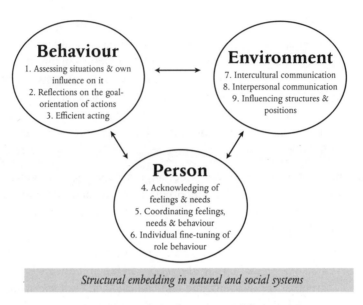

Figure 3.25 Nine basic competencies of changing (Donkers 2010, p.253; approved translation)

According to Donkers, the nine basic competencies are comprised of characteristics necessary to improve development processes and action abilities for individuals, groups, organizations, and communities, and therefore achieve change. 'The competencies are not formulated in objective, static endings. Every basic competency is open to elaboration. Besides that: other existing competency profiles can be incorporated' (pp.251–252, translation WB).

In Figure 3.25 outlining basic competencies of changing is intended as a framework for reflection. It 'can be used to identify and/or compare actions of clients, professionals, groups, and organizations, or as a heuristic in finding what is wise and virtuous in a particular situation' (p.252, translation WB).

The concept of self-regulation is a core element in Donkers' theory of changing. It refers to a different view on change and changing from the social-technological one of the Planned Change Theory. Self-regulation is a reflective (not a mechanical) process of value-oriented, intentional action that always takes place in a specific context.

Donkers' theory of changing is based on various ideals such as reflectivity, meaning, democratic attitude, inner balance, constancy in life, change of perspectives, thinking in terms of relation to others (instead of individualization or self), contributing to 'the good life', and balancing self-care and care for others. According to Donkers, his approach 'contains a personal and moral reflection that refers to a philosophical and principled justification for which he provides a conceptual framework' (p.274, translation WB). Donkers connects his normative stand with an open position. 'It is a moral approach, without moralization... It is true that it concerns value-oriented action, but values themselves are not creating desirable behaviour. In this sense, values have to be distinguished from standards' (p.274, translation WB).

I agree with Donkers that the concept of self-regulation, aimed at realization of essential human values, fits a broad, integrative approach that includes existing strategies of change and (therefore) goes beyond them. His theory is related to the holistic interactionism of Magnusson (as summarized in Section 2.3.1). Like Donkers, Magnusson emphasizes

> an approach to the individual and the person-environment system as organized wholes, functioning as integrated totalities. At each level, the totality derives its characteristic features and properties from the interaction among the elements involved, not from the effect of each isolated part on the totality. Each aspect of the structures and processes that are operating (perceptions, plans, values, goals, motives, biological factors, conduct, etc.), as well as each aspect of the environment, takes on meaning from the role it plays in the total functioning of the individual. (Magnusson 2000, pp.42–43)

Magnusson includes the role of the acting person in his concept of 'self-organization', while Donkers integrates it into the concept of 'self-regulation'. While Magnusson stays with his 'self-organization as guiding principle in developmental processes' (p. 43) on a theoretical level, Donkers attempts to work it out and modify it for use in social interventions.

It seems to me that the action concepts of 'self-organization' and 'self-regulation' are connected on an operational level, as Donkers (2011) demonstrated. Perhaps this can also be done on a theoretical level. As far as I can see, Magnusson's self-organization could be part of Donkers' concept of self-regulation.

Donkers' theory can be qualified as an open process theory, focused on essential values. Donkers describes his theory as 'a social-constructive approach that is based on a dynamic and competent way of handling facts and situations' (p.102, translation WB), combined with a systemic (i.e. complex theoretical) approach of changing.

It is suitable for social workers to utilize the Integrative Theory of Changing because of its social constructive approach and its elements congruent with the international definition of social work. These elements include social change, interaction, problem solving, empowerment, liberty, well-being in society, values of human rights and social justice, and interventions in accordance with these principles. Donkers' theory encompasses all of these elements. It is also important to note that this holistic approach is characteristic of both Integrative Theory of Changing and of social work.

In terms of Donkers' Integrative Theory of Changing, the core task of social workers is to empower people, organizations, and communities by (creating conditions for) strengthening their self-regulating abilities.

Social workers help vulnerable people in distress to improve their quality of life, thereby helping them to become contributing members of society. Thus, the support provided by social workers is crucial to the betterment of society and its overall functioning.

Donkers discusses the following conditions for stimulating self-regulation in society (pp.262–263):

- facilitating dialogical forms of demand-oriented working
- support of self-organized, practice-oriented social learning situations
- increasing the influence of citizens on policy development
- more space and better facilities for professionals in social institutions
- support for self-organization and self-control initiatives rather than bureaucratic control
- focus on improving the quality of social services
- greater trust in citizens and professionals.

I agree with the conditions outlined by Donkers above. They should all be a subject of social policy. In my opinion, the social work profession should support and maintain structural conditions for improving self-regulating abilities of people in the framework of a democratic functioning society with a high standard of quality of life for all. In Chapter 5, I will discuss the relationship between social work, citizenship, and the social and democratic functioning of society.

4.
Help and Support

In this chapter, I describe tasks, roles and the *action repertoire* of social workers. I begin by discussing the 13 internationally defined purposes of social work and place them within the goal and task-oriented framework of Pincus and Minahan (1973). By doing so, I embed these core purposes of social work into the broad professional context in which they function (Section 4.1). I discuss the various roles undertaken by social workers in order to successfully apply their developmental, action-oriented psychosocial approaches and interventions (Section 4.2). The ability to fulfil different roles is part of the action repertoire of social workers, which I define and explain in the last section (Section 4.3) of this chapter.

4.1 Purpose and tasks of social work

According to *Global Standards for the Education and Training of the Social Work Profession* (IFSW and IASSW 2004b), social work is focused on interventions for social support and on developmental, protective, preventive, and/or therapeutic purposes. To achieve this, social work has the following 13 *core purposes* (the numbering is mine, WB) (p.3):

1. Facilitate the inclusion of marginalized, socially excluded, dispossessed, vulnerable and at-risk groups of people.

2. Address and challenge barriers, inequalities and injustices that exist in society.

3. Form short and longer-term working relationships with and mobilize individuals, families, groups, organizations and communities to enhance their well-being and their problem solving capacities.

4. Assist and educate people to obtain services and resources in their communities.

5. Formulate and implement policies and programmes that enhance people's well-being, promote development and human rights, and promote collective social harmony and social stability, insofar as such stability does not violate human rights.

6. Encourage people to engage in advocacy in regards to pertinent local, national, regional and/or international concerns.

7. Act with and/or for people to advocate the formulation and targeted implementation of policies that are consistent with the ethical principles of the profession.

8. Act with and/or for people to advocate changes in those policies and structural conditions that maintain people in marginalized, dispossessed and vulnerable positions, and those that infringe the collective social harmony and stability of various ethnic groups, insofar as such stability does not violate human rights.

9. Work towards the protection of people who are not in a position to do so themselves, for example children and youth in need of care and persons experiencing mental illness or mental retardation, within the parameters of accepted and ethically sound legislation.

10. Engage in social and political action to impact social policy and economic development, and to effect change by criticizing and eliminating inequalities.

11. Enhance stable, harmonious and mutually respectful societies that do not violate people's human rights.

12. Promote respect for traditions, cultures, ideologies, beliefs and religions amongst different ethnic groups and societies, insofar as these do not conflict with the fundamental human rights of people.

13. Plan, organize, administer and manage programmes and organizations dedicated to any of the purposes delineated above.

This enumeration of core purposes covers most tasks of social workers, but needs some classification.

The 13 core purposes fit with Pincus and Minahan's task-oriented social work approach, as described in their world-renowned textbook, *Social Work Practice: Model and Method* (1973).

According to Pincus and Minahan, social work 'is concerned with the interactions between people and their social environment which affect the ability of people to accomplish their life tasks, alleviate distress, and realize their aspirations [interests] and values' (p.9). Examples of *life tasks* are: growing up, learning in school, working, marrying and rearing a family, and dealing with traumatic life situations if and when they arise.

Social work offers help to people who are hampered by the psychosocial conditions in their everyday life and struggle to fulfil their life tasks in a satisfying way.

According to Pincus and Minahan, the purpose of social work is to:

(A) enhance the problem solving and coping capacities of people, (B) link people with systems that provide them with resources, services and opportunities, (C) promote the effective and humane operation of these systems, and (D) contribute to the development and improvement of social policy. (1973, p.9 numbers replaced by letters, WB)

These four groups of tasks of social work are carried out on different levels: task A on a micro level, B between micro and meso levels, C on meso and macro levels, and D on a macro level.

The social worker has a particular role in each of the tasks:

- In task A, the social worker fulfils the role of educator.

- In task B, the social worker is intermediary and mediator.

- In task C, the social worker operates as organizational consultant.

- In task D, the social worker plays the role of sounding board and policy advisor.

(A more detailed description of these roles is given in Section 4.2.)

Figure 4.1 shows the connection between levels, tasks, and roles.

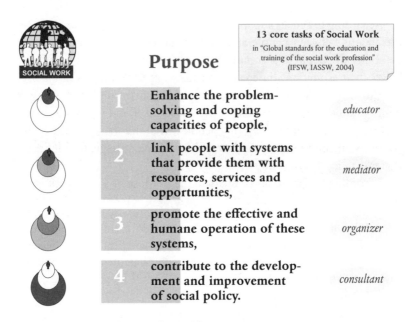

Figure 4.1 Purpose of social work according to Pincus and Minahan
(1973), extended with corresponding levels and roles

Pincus and Minahan focus on the societal tasks of social work. These are comprehensive tasks existing in a broad series of mutually connected activities on micro, meso and macro scales. These tasks include creating conditions for problem solving, forming groups, offering direct support to clients seeking help, and influencing the policies and procedures of institutions, organizations, and companies.

The 13 core purposes of social work can be classified under Pincus and Minahan's four tasks of social work as follows:

A. *Enhance the problem solving and coping capabilities of people*

3. Form short and longer-term working relationships.

8. Act with and/or for people to advocate changes in those policies and structural conditions that maintain people in marginalized, dispossessed, and vulnerable positions.

9. Work towards the protection of people who are not in a position to do so themselves.

11. Enhance stable, harmonious, and mutually respectful societies that do not violate people's human rights.

B. *Link people with systems that provide them with resources, services, and opportunities*

    4. Assist and educate people in obtaining services and resources in their communities.

C. *Promote the effective and humane operation of these social service systems*

    1. Facilitate the inclusion of marginalized, socially excluded, dispossessed, vulnerable, and at-risk groups of people.

    2. Address and challenge barriers, inequalities, and injustices that exist in society.

    6. Encourage people to engage in advocacy in regards to pertinent local, national, regional, and/or international concerns.

    13. Plan, organize, administer, and manage programmes and organizations dedicated to any of the purposes mentioned.

D. *Contribute to the development and improvement of social policy*

    5. Formulate and implement policies and programmes that enhance people's well-being, promote development and human rights, and promote collective social harmony and social stability, insofar as such stability does not violate human rights.

    7. Act with and/or for people to advocate the formulation and targeted implementation of policies that are consistent with the ethical principles of the profession.

    10. Engage in social and political action to impact social policy and economic development, and to effect change by critizizing and eliminating inequalities.

    12. Promote respect for traditions, cultures, ideologies, beliefs, and religions.

Pincus and Minnahan's definition of the purpose of social work is broad, but becomes more particular by differentiating this purpose into four groups of tasks. These groups of tasks cover all three levels in society (micro, meso, and macro) and refer to particular roles of the social worker.

    The four tasks overlap the three well-known specializations (the 'Major Methods') of social work developed during the first decennia of the 20th century: social casework (helping individuals and families), social group work (in many forms and settings), and community organization/

community development. These three specializations in social work stand as a practical division of tasks proven to be useful and functional, and still recognized in modern practice and education. Specialization within a profession is acceptable, even necessary and inevitable, as long as it is in accordance with common aspects and codes of conduct of the profession. By maintaining professional standards, getting a proper education and continuing one's competency, representing people and advocating in their best interest, offering quality service, practising with integrity, and maintaining good public relations, the social work profession can build and preserve a strong and respected position in society.

All the components mentioned above fit in the existing body of knowledge of social work. In my opinion, this is one of the reasons why Pincus and Minahan's textbook, first published in 1973, is still so well known and continues to be used as a textbook to educate social workers all over the world.

4.2 Roles

As described in the previous section, there are four task groups in social work, with characteristic roles of the social worker in each of them. These roles are *task-oriented roles* of the social worker.

A social worker is *teacher and coach* by helping clients cope more effectively and efficiently in everyday life, and by teaching clients how to use their abilities, and develop their skills to prevent and solve problems and to open new perspectives in their lives.

When a social worker refers and connects clients with available resources and support from various organizations and institutions, the social worker functions as *intermediary and mediator.*

Service organizations and institutions sometimes neglect their obligations to society, or do not provide sufficient resources to meet the basic needs of the population in which, and for which, they are functioning (and financed for). In these situations, social workers can act as *sounding board, advocate,* or *organization consultant.* Social workers have to decide how involved to become in the situation and how ardently to advocate depending on the characteristics and seriousness of the problems, the situation and position of the client(s), the institutional context, and the balance of powers.

If the social policy of an organization or a governmental body is lacking, social workers can initiate problem solving and make suggestions regarding solutions, with or without clients specifically requesting assistance. In these kinds of cases, the social worker functions as a *consultant* or *policy advisor*.

In addition to task-oriented roles, social workers also fill *process-oriented roles*, whereby the social worker intervenes in change processes of clients and actors in their environment. Depending on the specific situation, understanding of the client, and relationship with the client, the social worker can perform one or more roles with varying degrees of direct influence on the change process.

Figure 4.2 gives an overview of possible process-oriented roles of the social worker.

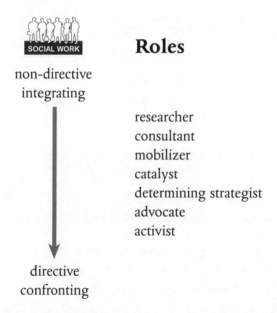

Roles

non-directive
integrating

researcher
consultant
mobilizer
catalyst
determining strategist
advocate
activist

directive
confronting

Figure 4.2 Roles of the social worker, from non-directive to directive

The figure shows possible, temporary, situation-specific roles of a social worker within the context of a working relationship with a client or clients, with whom and for whom the social worker carries out a goal-oriented programme or action plan. The roles are arranged on a scale from non-directive (integrating) to directive (confronting).

Choosing the appropriate role and timing of interventions is a matter of expertise and experience, depending on the knowledge, attitude, and skills of the professional worker. No matter what, the social worker should not take on roles that he is not competent to fill.

A role must be justified toward the client, the employer of the social worker, and society. A role requires expertise to perform it in a competent way. Performing a role is never the end goal, but rather is a means used to serve a particular purpose.

Along with task-oriented and process-oriented roles, *competence-oriented* roles also exist.

According to Zwart and Middel (2005), three basic forms of professionalism are required to handle and guide developmental processes: justification, purpose, and core competence. Underlying each of these forms of professionalism is a fundamental attitude in the form of expert, participant, and therapist (Figure 4.3).

Fundamental attitude	Justification	Purpose	Core competence
EXPERT	credibility	vision	authority
PARTICIPANT	presence	dialogue	confidence
THERAPIST	healing	interventions	care

Figure 4.3 Three basic forms of professionalism (based on Zwart and Middel 2005, p.108)

The ability to fulfil task-oriented, process-oriented, and competence-oriented roles is part of the *action repertoire* of a professional, in this case a social worker. Just as a theatre company has a repertoire (all plays one can perform), the helping professional also possesses an action repertoire which he can make use of if the need arises. This is the subject of the next section of this chapter.

4.3 Professional action repertoire

In the social work profession, goal and task setting imply the ability to act in an instrumental and strategic way, using good communication skills:

- *Instrumental action* is a form of rational goal-oriented action that attempts to influence change processes through an object-oriented, technical-instrumental method. Instrumental action fits in a social-technological change model. An example is Planned Change Theory, which is part of the body of knowledge of social work (see Sections 3.3 and 3.4).

- *Strategic action* is the social variant of goal-rational action. Strategic action includes the interaction between persons and environment, and takes into account the behaviour of other persons, groups, organizations, institutions, and communities involved. In critical variants, the societal context, which includes power, resources, and their distribution, is an important factor in analysis, planning, and implementation. Strategic action fits in a person-oriented change model as well as a society-critical model (see Section 3.4.4).

- *Communicative action* is focused on dialogue, transfer, and the achievement of mutual agreement on all levels, in every imaginable situation and toward all possible target groups and interested parties (see Section 2.5).

It is important to stress that none of these forms of professional action can be seen as separate from normative choices and the personality of the worker. Besides, professional action is always performed within a meaningful, sensitive context, in collaboration with others (clients, colleagues, and customers), and is based on the ethical code of the worker's profession.

According to Geert van der Laan (1993), 'different forms of action can exist abreast, without watering down the conceptual clarity' (p.50, translation WB). This is possible because in professional help practice, two levels of interaction exist side by side: 'a meta level of the definition of the situation, and an object level of actual help' (p.49, translation WB). For this reason, it is possible 'to bring instrumental and strategic action under communicative supervision' and 'to connect the search for truth, normativity and subjectivity with each other on a micro level' (p.5, translation WB).

I am of the opinion that these conclusions of van der Laan confirm the viability of Donkers' integrative theory for social work (see Section 3.4.5).

Professional action (instrumental, strategic, and communicative), professional roles (oriented on tasks, processes, and competencies), as well as personal view (of humankind, society, and development) are part of the *action repertoire* of the social worker.

The Dutch scientist Max van der Kamp, who passed away in July 2007, left us many valuable theories and concepts. He developed the following intelligent and useful definition of action repertoire:

The action repertoire of the helper includes particular heuristics [manners to discover and to invent, WB] and algorithms [methods of arguing and debating, WB], routines and intuitions, cognitive problem-solving skills and social-emotional strategies. These are based on knowledge and skills, learned through education or experience, and inspired by views of humankind, (sub)culture and vision of society. (van der Kamp 1993, p.8, translation WB)

Figure 4.4 summarizes van der Kamp's definition and description of action repertoire.

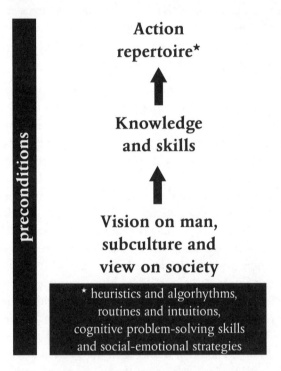

Figure 4.4 Developing an action repertoire in social work (based on van der Kamp 1993)

Before, during, and after their studies, students/workers are subjects of selection. Selection takes place before study because an individual's choice to study social work is influenced by particular values and standards and by the public image of the profession in society. Throughout their education period, students acquire knowledge and skills, develop their own vision, and acquire appropriate attitudes for working as a professional. At the conclusion of their studies, students are in possession of a basic action repertoire, which they can use to begin their practice as social workers.

The further development of a social worker's action repertoire depends on personal factors, continuing education and competency, specialized training, and on the preconditions in professional practice. Social workers' own efforts to update and improve their expertise and practice skills are determining factors in the extent, depth, effectiveness, and usefulness of the action repertoire of the working professional.

5.

Position and Functions of Social Work in Society

The position, tasks, and functions of social work in society are subject to continuing debate in scientific circles of social work. Emphasis is placed on the control functions of social work, on its emancipatory function, on its educational impact, or – and this seems to be the most realistic approach – on the dualistic character of the work. By dualistic, I mean controlling while emancipating, and emancipating while controlling. Doing the one thing implies the other. It is not possible to emancipate without having control over the interventions and change process, and vice versa. Social workers help groups and individuals to become aware of their position and circumstances, and refer them to organizations and institutions who are able to supply them with the resources they need. In turn, these governmental, non-governmental and commercial organizations have and maintain power over them and others within society.

To analyse and outline the societal position and functions of social work, I use relevant models and concepts of political sciences and public administration. In Section 5.1, social work is positioned as part of the social infrastructure in society. The profession is an important instrument of social policy and contributes to the improvement of the quality of life in society. In Section 5.2, I argue that social work is crucial in maintaining the democratic functioning of society. In many places, in many different ways, and on various levels, social workers stimulate and support citizen participation and empowerment. Section 5.3 contains a summary and overview.

5.1 Social work and social policy

In modern policy terms, used by the European Union, every society has a threefold infrastructure: an *economic infrastructure* (factories, offices, supermarkets, institutions, etc.), an *environmental-physical infrastructure* (roads, railways, canals, communication facilities, buildings, etc.) and a *social infrastructure*, defined as: 'the whole of organizations, services and provisions offering individual citizens in their own environment the possibilities to participate in society' (Tweede Kamer der Staten General 1999, p.2). Social work institutions are part of this social infrastructure.

The social infrastructure is directed and coordinated by the main financer: the government, according to goals, priorities, and allocation of means formulated in its *social policy*. From 1997 the traditional, (neo) liberal approach of social policy (dominated by economic policy and a top-down point of view) in Europe and its member states came under scientific pressure. It should make way, and is at last making way, for a modern, participative approach based on the concept of social quality.

5.1.1 Social quality

The idea of *social quality* was developed in the mid-1990s, following a series of scientific and policy-oriented meetings in Europe.

Social quality is defined as: 'the extent to which people are able to participate in the social and economic life and development of their communities under conditions which enhance their well-being and individual potential' (European Foundation on Social Quality 2012, p.1).

Social quality, as the key concept for a new social policy, was created

> as a reaction to (and possible antidote for) the longstanding subordination of social policy to economic policy. In the 1990s, this conflict was highly visible in the European Union (EU) as the convergence criteria for economic and monetary union resulted in reductions in social spending and increases in unemployment. The failure of social policy to counteract these developments, because of its unequal relationship with economic policy, called for a new approach aimed at establishing a balance between economic and social development. (European Foundation on Social Quality 2012, p.1)

The new approach to policy was supported by more than 1000 European scientists all over Europe in the so-called 'Amsterdam Declaration on the Social Quality of Europe, June 10 1997'. The Declaration begins with a principle statement:

> Respect for the fundamental human dignity of all citizens requires us to declare that we do not want to see growing numbers of beggars, tramps and homeless in the cities of Europe. Nor can we countenance a Europe with large numbers of unemployed, growing numbers of poor people and those who have only limited access to health care and social services.' (European Foundation on Social Quality 1997, p.1)

For the scientist 'these and many other negative indicators demonstrate the current inadequacy of Europe to provide social quality for all its citizens.' (p.1) 'In contrast' they want 'a European society that is economically successful, but which, at the same time, promotes social justice and participation for its citizens.' (p.1) According to the scientists

> This would be a Europe in which social quality is paramount. Its citizens would be able and required to participate in the social and economic life of their communities and to do so under conditions which enhance their well-being, their individual potential and the welfare of their communities. To be able to participate, citizens must have access to an acceptable level of economic security and of social inclusion, live in cohesive communities, and be empowered to develop their full potential. In other words, social quality depends on the extent to which economic, social and political citizenship is enjoyed by all residents of Europe. In a globalized economy competitiveness should go hand in hand with the promotion of social cohesion and the realization of the full potential of each European citizen. (p.1)

The Amsterdam Declaration on the Social Quality of Europe was starting point of the European Foundation on Social Quallity (EFSQ), a great initiator and 'spider in the web' of research projects and publications, serving the cause of a liveable, democratic Europe for all citizens.

Figure 5.1 shows social quality as the outcome of constant tensions in everyday life. The vertical line shows the tensions between the everyday life world of the individual citizen (biographical processes) and the societal processes on meso and macro levels. The horizontal axis represents the tensions between the system world (systems, institutions, organizations) and the life world (communities, groups, families).

Social Processes

socio-economic security   social cohesion

Social Quality

social inclusion   social empowerment

Systems
Institutions
Organisation

Communities
Groups
Families

Biographical processes

Figure 5.1 The quadrant of social quality (Herrmann and van der Maesen 2008, p.8)

Four basic conditions determine the opportunities for these processes or social relations to develop:

> People must have the capability to interact (*social empowerment*); the institutional and structural context must be accessible to them (*social inclusion*); they must have access to the necessary material and other resources that facilitate interaction (*socio-economic security*); and the necessary collective accepted values and norms, such as trust, that enable community building (*social cohesion*). In light of these considerations, social quality is defined as the extent to which people are able to participate in their social and economic life, and the development of their communities under conditions which enhance their well-being and individual potential. (Herrmann and van der Maesen 2008, pp.11–12)

The four basic conditions as mentioned are the constituting elements of social quality. They can be measured on an individual level by research, as follows (van der Maesen and Walker 2005, pp.12–13):

- *Socio-economic security:* the extent to which people have stable resources over time.

- *Social cohesion:* the extent to which social relations, based on identities, values and norms, are shared between individuals and groups.

- *Social inclusion:* the extent to which people have access to and are integrated into the different institutions and social relations that constitute everyday life.

- *Social empowerment:* the extent to which the personal capabilities of individual people and their ability to act are enhanced by social relations.

By measuring social conditions within a country, region, or local community, the extent or level of social quality can be determined, thereby indicating areas requiring improvement. The realization of this is the responsibility of government authorities in participation and cooperation with (organized) citizens.

Social quality as described above opened, at last, the 'social dimension' for policy makers. Social quality-based policy has the ability to implement an integrated approach, including the life world and participation of citizens, focusing on strengthening individual and social capacities and aiming for a better quality of life.

This new, integrated and participative way of policy making makes it easier to connect it to social work and to work with it in practice.

The connection with social work can also be made on the theoretical level. According to the theory of social quality.

> the social world is realized in the interaction (and interdependencies) between the self-realization of individual people as social beings and the formation of collective identities which occur in the context of both basic tensions. We call this the constitution of "the social."' (van der Maesen and Walker 2005, p.11)

Herrmann and van der Maesen (2008, pp.6–7) agree that

> the constitutive interdependency between processes of self-realization and processes of the formation of collective identities is a condition for 'the social', realized by the interactions of (i) actors, being – with their self-referential capacity – competent to act, and (ii) their framing structure, which translates immediately into the context of human relationships.

It is clear that the theory of social quality combines elements of two approaches that are also used by social workers: the ecological systems approach and the theory of communicative action (see Sections 2.4 and 2.5). And in my opinion it can also be connected with new approaches in social work like the integrative theory of change discussed in Chapter 3.

5.1.2 Local social policy

In many countries, there is a division of tasks in social policy between the authorities on national, regional, and local levels. In my country, the Netherlands, the division of tasks is as shown in Figure 5.2.

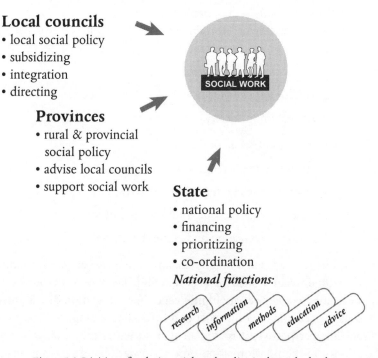

Local councils
- local social policy
- subsidizing
- integration
- directing

Provinces
- rural & provincial social policy
- advise local councils
- support social work

State
- national policy
- financing
- prioritizing
- co-ordination

National functions:

research   information   methods   education   advice

Figure 5.2 Division of tasks in social work policy in the Netherlands

As shown in the figure, social policy tasks in the Netherlands are divided over the three levels of authority as follows:

- Local governments finance and direct social institutions.

- Provincial governments advise local governments, support social workers, and are responsible for social policy in rural areas.

- The national government develops social policy, sets priorities, finances, coordinates, and supports a number of national institutions for research, information, development, education, and advice.

By decentralizing national power and resources, local governments develop social policy for their own territories within the framework of national legislation, regulations, and social policy. I refer to this as 'local social policy'.

Local social policy is the policy of a locality (place, district, region, or province) that concentrates on preventing and solving social problems, and creates the conditions which enable people to participate fully – politically and socially – in society.

According to Roelof Hortulanus (1997), a Dutch researcher and theorist of social policy, important motives for local social policy are:

- social justice and social cohesion
- self-help/self-sufficiency
- participation in society.

Core themes for local social policy are:

- protecting vulnerable persons and groups
- stimulating social integration and liveability
- generating start-up capital for creation of jobs
- support for recreation and cultural activities.

Local policy of any kind (not only social) is a sensitive subject in countries with a totalitarian system or a developing democracy. Resources and policy in these countries are highly centralized to control developments and initiatives, and to ensure that power remains among the ruling elite. From this perspective, it is evident that decentralization of policy was a priority in the transformation process toward democracy and market economy in the former communist countries of Eastern Europe.

As an example of decentralization of power and policy in the Netherlands, the long-existing practice of local social policy moved ahead quickly as a result of the Social Support Act (*Invoering WMO* 2008) introduced in 2007. *Social support* is a broad term for all professional and voluntary activities and services that are available for citizens to access in order to participate in society. The Social Support Act replaced existing legislation for social work, health prevention, care institutions, and provisions for elderly, disabled, and chronically ill patients, in an effort to increase the effectiveness and efficiency of social institutions and services, and to stop the growing public expenditure for social services (Netherlands Ministry of Health, Welfare and Sport 2011).

The *aim* of the Social Support Act is participation of all citizens in all facets of society. The *purpose* of the Social Support Act is to stimulate individual responsibility and mutual solidarity of citizens, through accessible social support at a community level.

The Act has to open in a perspective on a coherent policy in the field of social support and related areas. Services and resources are offered to empower individuals and groups by stimulating cooperation and coherence within communities.

Social support activities are actions in the following nine fields (Staatsblad 2010, pp.1–2):

1. The promotion of social cohesion and quality of life in villages, districts and neighbourhoods;

2. Prevention-focused support for young people experiencing problems with growing up and parents experiencing problems raising their children;

3. The provision of information, advice and client support;

4. Supporting volunteers and caregivers. This includes helping to find effective solutions if caregivers are temporarily unable to carry out their tasks;

5. The promotion of participation in society and independent functioning of people with a disability or chronic mental problem, and people with psychosocial problems;

6. The provision of services for people with a disability or chronic mental problem and people with psychosocial problems in order for them to be able to maintain and enhance their independence and participation in society;

7. The provision of social relief, including women's refuge and the pursuit of policies to combat acts of violence committed by a person from the victim's domestic circle;

8. The promotion of public mental health care…;

9. The promotion of policy regarding individuals with addictions.

The purpose, aim, and various fields within this new local social policy include the four basic conditions for social quality as discussed in Section 5.1.1.

The Dutch Social Support Act is an effort to cope with needs and problems using modern methods within the (local) social infrastructure. It can be considered as a broad social and administrative experiment.

Thus far, experiences have been mixed. A positive effect of the new local social policy is that local governments now have the opportunity to develop a cohesive policy on social support, living, and welfare, along with other related matters. Because of the possibility for participation by (organized) citizens in planning and programming, there is room for a bottom-up approach and democratic proceedings. However, problems with the availability and quality of some services, especially in family care, care for the elderly, and day care for children are some of the negative effects of local social policy. This is the result of neoliberal elements in the form of market mechanisms through public procurement of activities, competition, and dominating management in institutions.

It will take time and great effort for all participating actors to become used to this new manner of (local) policy development and implementation.

Figure 5.3 contains a summary of the subjects and their mutual relations described in this chapter.

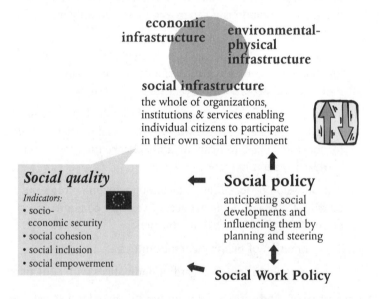

Figure 5.3 Place and functions of social policy and social work in society

The figure shows the threefold infrastructure in society: the *economic infrastructure* (factories, offices, supermarkets, institutions, etc.), the *environmental-physical infrastructure* (roads, railways, canals, communication facilities, buildings, etc.), and the *social infrastructure* (the whole of organizations, services, and provisions offering individual citizens the opportunity to participate in society from within the context of their own environment).

The *social infrastructure* of a country, region, or local community is government-directed by means of *social policy* and with financial support based on these social policies. The objective of social policy is to improve and maintain the *social quality of life* for all citizens in society. The extent of urgency, necessity, and success of social policies can be measured using the four indicators of social quality: socio-economic security, social cohesion, social inclusion, and social empowerment.

5.2 Social work and democracy

Social work makes a significant contribution to the democratic functioning of society because of the character of its work (supporting change), its purpose (enhancing well-being), how it works (stimulating empowerment and participation), and its specific role in the social infrastructure (monitoring, advising, and developing).

Democratic functioning refers to democracy in a broad sense, as it relates to the behaviour and actions of citizens, companies, institutions, and authorities, and their mutual influence and responsibility within society. In this respect, as stated in Section 1.2, democracy is 'the belief in freedom and equality between people, or a system of government based on this belief, in which power is either held by elected representatives or directly by the people themselves' (Cambridge Dictionaries Online 2011).

To determine the position of social work in the democratic process in society I have to researched in the fields of political science, public administration, and sociology. In an effort to avoid unnecessary theoretical exercises, I have found a connection between these disciplines on a strategic and instrumental level. I use the well-known cyclic political system model of the American political scientist David Easton, modified and extended by van de Gevel and van de Goor (1989). By adding contemporary concepts and theories about policy, decision making, and public administration to Easton's model, van de Gevel and van de Goor constructed a more comprehensive and useful model that has the character of (what I prefer to call) a *democratic policy and decision model.*

The democratic policy and decision model is suitable for demonstrating how social workers in various stages support the process of policy and decision making, by acting according to their training and profession. The model can be demonstrated particularly well using visual aids. I therefore include my own diagrams below, based on those of van de Gevel and van de Goor.

5.2.1 Democratic policy development and decision making

The American political scientist David Easton (see van de Gevel and van der Goor 1989) considers the state to be a vital part of a broader political system, working to maintain open, mutual relations with society.

Similar to other organizations, approached as open systems, the political system has an input, a throughput, and an output. This becomes a feedback loop where the output finds its way back into the political system in the form of new input based on evaluations of the success or potential of the output. Figure 5.4 demonstrates Easton's cyclic political system model.

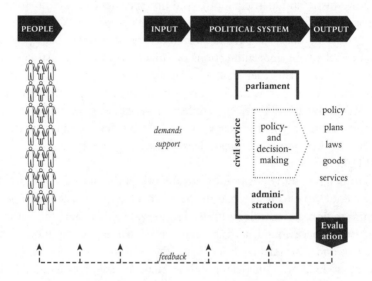

Figure 5.4 The cyclic political system model of David Easton (based on the summary by van de Gevel and van de Goor 1989, pp.78–86)

Easton's model emphasizes the *political system*, with a *parliament*, an *administration*, and *civil service* as important constituents. The *input* of the political system is formed by demands and support of the people, the citizens of the state. *Demands* are based on needs and desires, and express citizens' opinions of what the political system should do or not do. *Support* is related to satisfaction with the output of the political system through analysing positive and negative outcomes and measuring values and standards, balanced with upbringing, experience, and education.

The *input* that reaches the political system becomes a part of the process of *policy and decision making*, which in turn is transformed into *output*. The *output* of the political system includes policy, plans, laws, goods, and services for social groups, communities, organizations, companies, and institutions (van de Gevel and van de Goor 1989, Chapter 5). Evaluation of the political output creates a connection with potential new input, thereby creating a feedback loop within society whereby the cycle starts again from the beginning.

As previously stated, Easton emphasizes in the cyclic process of policy making the political system, not the social processes, developments and movements that produce new input based on earlier output of the system. For this and other reasons, my Dutch colleagues van de Gevel and van de Goor extended and adapted Easton's cyclic open political system model by adding a contemporary policy and actor approach. This resulted in a comprehensive, dynamic model with greater emphasis on the society of which the political system is part. The extended and adapted version of Easton's cyclic political system model is illustrated in Figure 5.5.

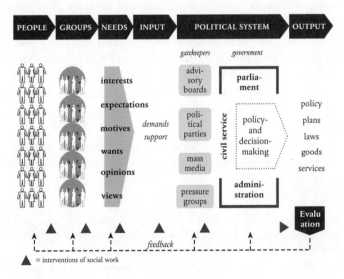

Figure 5.5 Democratic policy and decision model (based on van de Gevel and van de Goor 1989, supplemented with intervention points of social work)

As the diagram shows, van de Gevel and van de Goor outlined the *input* of the political system by including the prior social stages of *groups* (forming new groups and activating existing ones), and *needs* (articulating common needs, desires, and interests) resulting in *input* (demands and support) for the political system. Van de Gevel and van de Goor also added contemporary *gatekeepers* to the political system: advisory bodies, political parties, mass media, and by pressure groups.

The *interventions of social work* on the bottom row is my addition; neither Easton nor van de Gevel and van de Goor included social work in their models.

In the next section, I explain the contribution of social work to the stages of the democratic policy development and decision-making process in society.

5.2.2 Tasks and roles of social work in the democratic process

Although social work falls outside their specific scope of public administration, van de Gevel and van de Goor (1989) use terminology directly linked to common concepts and theories in social work. Forming of groups, articulation of common needs and interests, translation into demands and support for the political system, pressure groups, and feedback are all concepts in public administration as well as in social work.

Public administration, political science, and social work share some knowledge between their professional bodies and use familiar concepts originating from Planned Change Theory such as development, change, interaction, interventions, empowerment, steering, liberation, power, and balance.

In social work, the democratic policy development and decision cycle help maintain and continue the process of social development and change on macro and meso levels. This process creates new problems and vulnerable groups on one hand, and offers new chances for problem solving and empowerment on the other. Every stage of the cycle requires a different approach and set of activities to support development toward the next stage.

The democratic policy and decision model makes it possible to determine the position and functions of social work in each stage of the process.

Social work provides services in all six stages of the democratic policy and decision model, namely:

1. Stimulating and motivating individual citizens to organize, empower themselves, and participate.

2. Identifying individual needs as needs of a social group, and the forming and building of groups.

3. Articulating common needs of social groups.

4. Translating needs/interests into demand and support toward the political system.

5. Influencing political decision making.

6. Feeding back on decisions concerning social groups.

All of these stages are points of intervention for social work (see Figure 5.5). The interventions are social interventions in various forms, such as assistance, support, counselling, training, information, interest organization, articulation of needs, mediation, development, planning, programming, research, monitoring, and consultancy.

All these interventions are linked to processes of planned change through dialogue with clients. The interventions are directed at clients' interaction with their environment and important actors in that environment, influenced by underlying social structures and cultures.

The interventions are related to appropriate professional roles of the social worker. As *participator*, the social worker helps vulnerable individuals and families (social casework), groups (social group work), and communities (community work) to participate in and contribute to their micro, meso, and macro environments.

Through active participation, individual people and groups integrate with other people, forming a cohesive society with common values and standards. This is why a social worker can be referred to as an *integrator*.

In sociological terms, it can be argued that social work in all its forms and on all levels of operation contributes to the realization and preservation of a balance of powers in society (the term 'balance of powers' is from the American sociologist C. Wright Mills). The social worker acts as an equalizer, a *balancer* between different (members of) social groups and between citizens and institutions.

5.2.3 The democratic need for a balance of powers

Social workers generally operate within a network of individuals, groups, organizations, and communities, with each having its own means and methods to strengthen its position and achieve its goals. It is the art of the social work profession to provide support for clients within this societal arena without evoking unnecessary resistance or threatening the credibility and position of the profession.

Figure 5.6 shows the course and function of social work support through empowering clients and integrating clients' participation in the process.

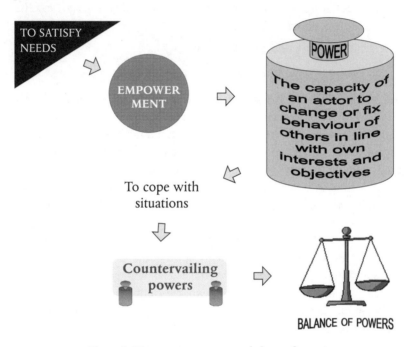

Figure 5.6 Empowerment to create a balance of powers

If an individual, family, social group, or community is not able to *satisfy vital needs* and *basic desires* in its environment, they can ask for help. It is the social worker's task to provide support and strength by helping clients tap into their own resources and abilities throughout the process of improving problematic circumstances. In social work, this process is called *empowerment*, or liberation. Feeling strong and having well-developed coping skills enables clients to *cope with situations* and have greater control of their own situation and problems arising over the course of their life. It is crucial for the significance of empowerment to be realized in the competitive atmosphere of market societies, where *power* is a dynamic phenomenon, defined as the capacity of an actor to change or fix behaviour of others in line with one's own interests and objectives.

If individual persons, groups, organizations, and communities are able to protect their own interests and to fight for their own rights, they are in a better position to have their vital needs and desires met. If a majority of people in society is able to achieve empowerment despite countervailing powers, an acceptable balance of powers can be created and maintained.

The strength and vitality of a democracy are dependent on a balance of powers in society; a balance that has to be created, reviewed, maintained and updated continuously. This is the reason why a democratic society needs to be proactive in providing opportunities, resources, and means – to keep its own system alive. In this respect having a system of social work which involves and empowers all citizens demonstrates attention and care for democratic functioning of society, its institutions, and its citizens.

5.3 Overview

Figure 5.7 provides a summary of the relationship between societal developments, social problems, social infrastructure, social policy, social work, citizen participation and public support. As part of the social infrastructure and as an instrument of social policy, the social work profession has a specific position and fulfils various roles.

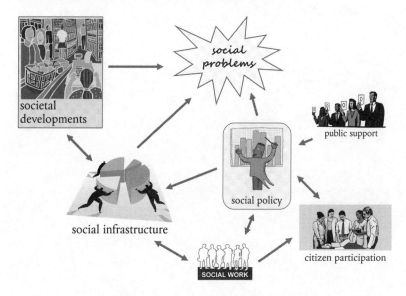

Figure 5.7 Map of the relationship between societal developments, social problems, social infrastructure, social policy, social work, citizen participation and public support

The map begins in the upper left corner with the *societal developments* initiated and fed by powerful forces of change: technology, economic activity, knowledge, religion and beliefs, and social lifestyle. These developments have both positive and negative effects on the quality of people's lives, depending on social group membership and where people live.

The various institutions that form the *social infrastructure* (education, health care, social work, sports, recreation, etc.) adjust to societal developments for the purpose of managing, reducing, or solving negative effects and social problems. To achieve this, social institutions make use of modern means, resources, facilities, and approaches.

Social institutions depend on government *social policy* and public means that the government is willing to spend on social infrastructure. Government social policies also dictate how and on what public money is spent. However, in a democratic society social policy and policy development are subject to public *support* and *citizen participation*.

Social work is part of the social infrastructure. It fulfils a variety of tasks, roles, and needs within society. Social work also contributes to the realization and improvement of social policy, promotes empowerment and participation of citizens, and contributes to the progress and quality of democratic policy development and decision making. Therefore, social work holds a distinct and significant position within the social infrastructure of society.

6.

Perspectives

This last chapter contains elements of a critical view on the development and future of social work. Section 6.1 includes a brief description of the historical development of social work. In Section 6.2, I define and discuss the process of globalization and its impact on social developments. Section 6.3 discusses the effects of neoliberal social policy on the social infrastructure, of which social work institutions are part. Using the Netherlands as an example, I discuss the effects of commercial management, market mechanisms, and output financing on the workers in social work, health care, and education (Section 6.3.1). I also pay attention to the growing critics and international movements (Section 6.3.2), ending up in Section 6.3.3 with a brief review and some conclusions. The last section of the book (Section 6.4) is dedicated to a 'democratic' way out and to a 'professional' way forward. It is time to 're-socialize' our social institutions, and to be part, as a profession, of the growing democratic and ecological awareness all over the world.

6.1 Development of social work

Developments from the past have influenced social work as we know it today. In order to broaden horizons and improve future processes, it is necessary to have knowledge and understanding of the recent history of professional social work.

The establishment of the first schools of social work in the 1890s is usually regarded as the starting point of professional social work. At that time, the Industrial Revolution was in full swing in the 'Old World' (Europe) as well as in the New World (USA, Canada, Australia, etc.). Rapid technological developments, mass production and transport, migration from rural to urban areas, and formation of new social classes were concrete, visible phenomena of a new era representing promise for change.

Other important events associated with that era were the labour and civil rights movements, as well as a growing impact of the major

149

ideologies: liberalism, socialism, conservatism, and (in European countries) Christian democracy.

Against this backdrop, the need for professional assistance in the sectors of health care and social care became manifest. Additionally, the conditions and resources needed to provide this support were identified.

Figure 6.1 shows in broad lines the development of professional social work from 1900 until today.

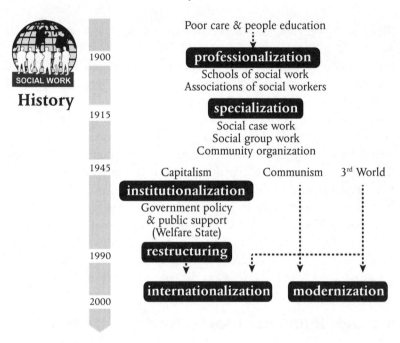

Figure 6.1 A broad history of professional social work

In 1898, the first school for social work, 'Summer School in Philanthropic Work', started in New York. In 1904, the school's name was changed to 'New York School of Philanthropy', and was changed again in 1917 to 'New York School of Social Work'. In 1963, the school was given its present name: 'Columbia University School of Social Work' (Wikipedia 2011). The first school in Europe was established in Amsterdam, the Netherlands, in 1899. Its name was 'Opleidingsinrichting voor Socialen Arbeid' (Educational Institution for Social Work) (van Gent 1991). In 1903 the name was changed to 'School voor maatschappelijk werk' (School for Social Work) (van Gent 1991).

The establishment of social work education institutes is preceded by, and the result of, centuries of care for the poor and educating people.

In 2008, the *British Journal of Social Work* published a special edition entitled 'Looking back while moving forward: Historical perspectives in social work'. The purpose of this edition was 'to take stock and reflect on the complex past from which the present has emerged' (Skehill 2008, p.619). The special edition included articles from British and foreign authors regarding the history of social work in their respective countries.

The 20th century demonstrates a relatively rapid emergence of professional social work in industrialized capitalist countries in and outside of Europe. This is directly connected to increasing state interference with society, for instance by means of social legislation. As in education and health care, social work developed areas of specialization within the profession. In the 1920s and 1930s, social work in the USA developed and adapted the Three Major Methods of Social Work: social casework (individual or family help), social group work (in various forms and different settings), and community organization (community work, development, and planning). In the United Kingdom, specialization led in the 1930s to separation between social casework and community education (i.e. community work). In other countries during that time-frame, there were varying periods of drifting apart and rapprochement between social casework, community work, and (in Europe) pedagogical work (social work with children) depending on the political-societal situation in each country.

As a reaction to the Great Depression in the 1930s, the Second World War, Communism, and the labour movement (labour unions and political parties), many of the Westernized countries of the Old and New World developed the so-called *Welfare State.*

According to the sociologist Thoenis the Welfare State is 'a system of public care that guarantees collective welfare, while maintaining the capitalistic production system, based on democracy' (van de Gevel and van de Goor 1989, p.46, translation WB). *Collective welfare* includes social benefits, subsidies, and provisions; private property and free market are characteristics of the *capitalistic production system; parliamentary democracy* is the most common form of democracy.

The Welfare State offers accessible systems of education, health care, social care, and social benefits for all citizens, financed by the state from tax revenues and premiums. In most Western countries there was, and still is, wide public support for this kind of collective care and societal organization.

Within the framework of the Welfare State, professional social work expanded quickly, just like education and health care. The institutionalization in the 1950s, 1960s, and 1970s resulted in an extensive system of specialized institutions and social workers. During this period, social work was a very popular field of study, because of a change in society's mentality toward a climate of social change.

The Welfare State became a historical success story. It functioned as an ideal model for many oppressed citizens of communist countries and poor people in developing countries. The Welfare State was and is a successful compromise between socialism and liberalism/capitalism (joined by Christian democratic parties in some of the European countries), in which socialism coincides with collective services, and liberalism is associated with free market, profit, and competition; both ideologies are bound by a parliamentary-democratic political system.

In the 1980s, the Welfare State was at risk of being sunk by its own success. It was easily accessible by all citizens and employers while there was too little coordination of providing institutions, from which too many were managed in a questionable way. As a result, costs increased exponentially. Many public scandals, followed by investigation and research, showed evidence of escalating misuse and abuse of provisions, subsidies, and benefits, as well as ineffective and inefficient service delivery and a lack of cooperation and coordination between agencies and organizations.

Cost figures from the Netherlands illustrate increasing expenditures for the collective sector after 1945: from 32 per cent of the Net National Income in 1950, to 39 per cent in 1960, 48 per cent in 1970, 65 per cent in 1980, and an inconceivable 70.5 per cent in 1985 (van de Gevel and van de Goor 1989).

In the 1980s, 'The Crisis of the Welfare State' became a recurring subject of public debate in almost all countries with such a system. To freeze and reduce the costs of the Welfare State, governments (with the British one in front) began using the 'scourge of the market' (privatization, market mechanisms, and commercially oriented management) to restructure public and social institutions. The negative repercussions of these operations are still felt today (see Section 6.3 and 6.4).

In the 1990s, globalization processes gained strength in the social field. Due to the fall of Communism in 1989 and the economic upswing of industrial production in Asia and Latin America, many countries were confronted with a need to modernize their social infrastructure. Advanced information and transportation technology, as well as the large number of international social service institutions, funds, and federations, made it easier than ever before to meet the needs of these countries.

These developments also affected social work and put pressure on the professional group to intensify existing mutual international contacts and to profile and present the social work profession on the global stage.

Today, the dominating neoliberal ideology is diminishing because of the worldwide financial crisis, environmental scandals, and managers who are filling their own pockets in public and social institutions. The upcoming global democratic and ecological movements need time to develop new, contemporary views and ideas, leading to new paradigms and ideologies. In the meantime, many citizens, interest groups, political parties, and authorities will continue struggling with the elementary dilemmas of making choices between personal and public interests, self-care and care for others, private consumption and public expenditure.

I have no doubt John Harris (2008) agrees with this rough historical analysis of professional social work. With British history specifically in mind, he concludes:

> Social work is often seen as a straightforward response to self-evident human needs and problems or as the outcome of 'professional projects' pursued by social workers. However, consideration of social work's history suggests that it is a contingent activity, conditioned by and dependent upon the context from which it emerges and in which it engages. The contingent nature of social work is considered by locating it within the context of five historical 'moments' that have had significant implications for social work's profile and practice... Review of these historical moments shows that welfare regimes are key in shaping the manner in which social work is constituted and enacted. Furthermore, aspects from each historical moment have been carried forward into present day social work; the construction of the present always owes something to moments from the past. (Harris 2008, pp.662–679: in his summary of the article)

6.2 Globalization

Globalization is the process by which regional (or national) economies, societies, and cultures are becoming integrated through a global network of communication, transportation, and trade. This process is being driven by a combination of economic, technological, sociocultural, political, and biological factors. Globalization also includes migration of people and the transnational circulation of ideas, languages, and popular culture through acculturation (Wikipedia 2011).

Globalization dates back to the early stage of (commercial) capitalism in the 16th century. The Industrial Revolution of the 19th and 20th centuries boosted and extended the globalization process. Globalization continued after 1945, and developed its modern characteristics in the 1960s. Terms such as 'The Global Village' and 'The Information Society' are characteristics of the contemporary state of the globalization process. Because globalization was, and still is, dominated by capitalism and the American culture and lifestyle, it is also referred to as 'Americanization'.

Existence of a world market of goods, services, labour and capital, is part and parcel of the globalization process. The world market is exploited and dominated by multinational companies, big banks, and powerful groups of private investors and speculators. For this reason, and as consequence of the tragedy of both world wars, governments were forced to create and support more intensive international cooperation.

Today, many former national tasks and responsibilities are delegated to supranational organizations including the United Nations (UN), the European Union (EU), NAFTA, NATO, World Bank, International Monetary Fund (IMF), and the International Labour Organization (ILO). These global civil and regulatory institutions rule the world with, and on behalf of, national governments. These organizations are necessary to prevent, limit, and solve major conflicts and crises worldwide.

The continuing, irreversible process of globalization has been penetrating more often and more deeply into regional, national, and local communities. The resulting changes offer new opportunities, but at the same time create new problems.

According to Michael Warren (2006), 'today's global capitalism affects all nations policy-wise, and all people in these nations consciousness-wise' (p.1). As a theologist he is of the opinion that 'in such a situation it seems necessary for religious people to be able to think consciously about the global money system and to talk back to it' (p.1).

Many authors share a critical opinion on the globalization process. According to Penna, Paylor, and Washington (2000), globalization has a strong impact on the social dimensions of well-being, social policy, and social practices. 'The developing global frameworks in economics, politics, communications, and social theory force all epistemic communities, academic and professional, to take note of the global context' (pp.109–110).

The authors address a special message to social work:

Social work as currently constituted is framed largely in the cultural context of the nation in which it is practiced. As we enter a new century, such nationally framed practice is unable to cope with social and economic trends that are global in dimension. Transformations in political economy have generated problems of social exclusion and poverty that affect all countries to greater or lesser degrees' (Penna *et al.* 2000, p.110).

This is preceded by the warning that 'the social polarization and the potential and actual social disorder they produce are conditions of modern living that transcend individual nations. (p.110).

The penetrating globalization process generates comparable social circumstances in different countries, intensified by neoliberal policy of deregulation, liberalization, and privatization of national governments, as required by international institutions such as the World Bank and IMF. This occurs in exchange for loans and financial assistance.

It is difficult for nationally organized social institutions to cope with social and economical developments of international character and origin. According to Penna *et al.* (2000), 'it is time to think globally about social work and consider how professional social work can develop political and practice intervention strategies that can adequately react to these circumstances at a transnational level' (p.110).

Although social work, like many other professions, is organized and financed on a national level, it is expected that international contacts and cooperation between institutions and workers will continue and increase because of ongoing globalization. For example, more policies (including in the social field) will be developed and monitored on a supranational level by governing bodies like the European Union.

Penna *et al.* wrote their article in 2000, on the doorstep of the 21st century. Their article held great foresight. Today, social work is present and stronger than ever before on the global stage. The international reins have been drawn more tightly and result in international documents and declarations affecting the profession. Thanks to the internet, these documents and declarations are widely distributed and better known than ever before in the international history of social work.

The following outline gives an overview of contemporary international presence and activities of social work. It is not complete; however, it provides an impression.

6.2.1 International organizations

Social workers are organized in the International Federation of Social Workers (IFSW) with regional and national branches. Social work teachers meet and participate in the International Association of Schools of Social Work (IASSW) with regional branches such as the European Association of Schools of Social Work (EASSW). The International Consortium for Social Development (ICSD) is an organization of practitioners, scholars, and students in the human services sector. Another important, long-existing global player is the International Council on Social Welfare (ICSW) that supports improvement of well-being, social development, and social justice in the world. More information about these organizations can be found in Healy and Hall (2007).

6.2.2 International journals and magazines

There are many international social work journals and magazines of which I recommend: *European Journal of Social Work*, *Journal of Social Work Education*, and the *Community Development Journal*. There are also magazines online such as *The New Social Worker Online* (www. socialworker.com), The International Online Journal *Social Work & Society* (www.socwork.net), and the related *SW&S News Magazine* (www. socmag.net). Also interesting are the *British Journal of Social Work* (www3. oup.co.uk/social), *Australian Social Work* (www.tandf.co.uk/journals/ titles/0312407X.asp) and *The Journal of Social Intervention: Theory and Practice* (www.journalsi.org). Wayne State University offers an extensive overview of e-journals on social welfare and social work at www.lib. wayne.edu/resources/journals.

6.2.3 Data banks and portals on the internet

The internet contains many data banks and portals on social work. For example: the *Social Work Access Network* (www.cosw.sc.edu/swan – access required), the *New Social Worker Online* (www.socialworker.com), and the *Social Work Café* (www.socialworkcafe.net).

6.2.4 Books

Numerous book publications regarding social work history and present activities exist, many in the English language, and some are available in translated versions. In addition, there is a long-established, extensive *Encyclopaedia of Social Work* in the English language. Its 20th edition was published in 2008 (Mizrahi and Davids 2008). It is also available in a digital version.

6.3 Neoliberal social policy

The crisis of the Welfare State in the 1980s, and the collapse of Communism at the end of that decade, mark a huge societal shift, especially in Western countries. The era of the Cold War, emancipation, democratization, youth culture, labour and civil rights, neo-Marxism, anti-war, and alternative lifestyles shifted into an era of neoliberalism, neocapitalism, civil society, the rise of China and India, the digital revolution, mobility, terrorism, globalization, mixing up of cultures, spiritualism, and ecology.

Neoliberal social policy fits into the new societal climate from the 1990s, based on the idea of individual responsibility by each citizen. In a neoliberal society, the government withdraws itself and takes a step back, by privatizing public institutions and services, or subjecting them to market mechanisms and commercial management. In doing so, the government reduces its own responsibilities to (co)financing, facilitation, and monitoring.

To address the crisis of the welfare state in their respective countries in the 1980s most governments followed the example of the British government under the Conservative Prime Minister Margaret Thatcher, by implementing a neoliberal social policy of deregulation, liberalization, and privatization. The 'scourge of the market' had to discipline the social institutions in order to make them more efficient and cooperative, and to limit the introduction of costly subsidies, services, and benefits.

Commercial management and the implementation of market mechanisms in education, health care and social care are specific, limited forms of privatization. In its most radical form, privatization is disposing of public tasks to the free market by selling them to the highest bidder(s) and/or securing them in commercial companies, quoted on the stock exchange. The objective is to improve the efficiency, effectiveness, and market orientation of services and provisions. Examples of relatively successful radical forms of privatization are postal and telephone services, cable and internet services, railways, buses and tramways, power supply, and water supply.

The British social worker and sociologist John Harris published a sobering book in 2003, *The Social Work Business*, regarding the privatization in the United Kingdom under 'Iron Lady' Margaret Thatcher, and the effects on social work services. Harris describes how a new social group of managers was formed on the waves of neoliberalism and American management theories which penetrated public and nonprofit institutions. The new class of managers quickly developed into a pedantic elite, because they were not open to feedback or criticism. This was in accordance with the ideological mood of the time, with social technology (business management, public management, and organization theory) and a universal belief of managers' ability to supervise everything and everyone. In this respect, I often refer to a favourite statement of one of the directors I know, in whose opinion 'there is no difference between managing a factory and a local social institution' (*sic*!).

In the UK, successive Conservative governments implemented an expansive policy of privatization and implementing market mechanisms in the public and social sector. To a certain extent, this was followed by British Commonwealth countries such as Canada, Australia, and New Zealand. On the European continent, the Netherlands became the promoter of neoliberal policy. Social pedagogic scientists from Germany criticized this development in order to resist it, and used to refer to the Netherlands as the springboard for the Anglo-Saxon model.

The German reference to the Dutch was accurate. Dutch politics followed in the 1980s Thatcher's approach in the UK, and opted for the discipline of the market by implementing a neoliberal social policy with less governmental involvement and more market and enterprise. There was little protest, because of the division between specialized social workers and a lack of intellectual opposition. Any efforts to resist were undermined and stifled from the beginning by referring to the economic recession at that time, and creating a generally negative image of social services and social workers.

In the 1980s, the Dutch government implemented six long-term operations to manage the Welfare State (van de Gevel and van de Goor 1989, pp.65–71). These so called *major operations* were:

1. Reconsideration of public services. No longer providing care and services from infancy until death. Emphasis on individual responsibility of citizens.

2. Decentralization of government. More control and funding from the national level redistributed at the provincial and local levels.

3. Privatization of public services, implementation of market mechanisms in nonprofit institutions, and a shift from input to output financing in health care, social care, and education.

4. Deregulation. Reducing laws and regulations. Placing more responsibility on citizens and private initiatives.

5. Reorganization of the national government, resulting in a smaller, more efficient political system.

6. Reduction in the number of civil servants.

This long-term policy resulted in an assortment of positive and negative effects for education, health care and social care that still resonate today. Institutions were forced into mergers and upgrades. Managers, mainly from outside the profession(s), set economic goals, introduced market mechanisms, and increased productivity, leading to new and more bureaucracy. The financing government changed the system of subsidies into output financing based on 'hard' production figures and facts.

Drawing 3 The social worker as marionette of the market (© Henny Feijer)

6.3.1 Market, management, and profession

Many of the social institutions in Western countries have upgraded to larger units since the 1990s, and are now directed by managers and run like companies. In this section, I discuss the consequences for professional workers and the services provided in health care and social work. The Netherlands serves as a practical example.

In the 1990s and the beginning of the new millennium, leading public officials and employers of health care, social care, and education in the Netherlands were impassioned by the new capitalist spirit. Many directors of social and care institutions started to present themselves as social entrepreneurs, running their institutions as a company, operating on a market, and making cost/benefit analysis to offer attractive, competitive products and services, not only financed by the government, but also paid for by institutions, commercial companies and individual customers.

This approach in economic terms of social work, health care and education is a curious mix of assumptions, facts, and wishful thinking. Almost all institutions that are part of the social infrastructure are still financed today for 80 per cent or more by public means, both directly (by local, provincial and national governments) and indirectly (by police, judicial authorities, hospitals, housing corporations, etc.). Despite what managers think or say: social work and social care are still paid from the public purse, just as health care, education and many cultural institutions are.

Since the middle of the 1990s, implementation of commercial-industrial work methods in social institutions has been criticized by two of the few authentic thinkers on health care and social work in the Netherlands: Harry Kunneman and Andries Baart. Both scientists operated from within philosophical, normative circles (i.e. the Humanistic University and the Catholic University in Utrecht), in which objectivity in critical reflection is imperative. The situation in the Netherlands is typical in that it took many years before a wider group of intellectuals and professional workers integrated the critical line of Kunneman's and Baart's thinking. Because of this an early effort, in 1998, by Taco Brandsen to start a discussion on 'managerialism' (see further in this section) failed.

According to Kunneman (1996), since the end of the 1980s workers in social institutions have been confronted 'with a new, output-oriented management style, in which the financier is the customer and workers provide clients with services in as little time as possible, with maximum efficiency' (p.107, translation WB). This is not without consequences: 'There are more checks and control on the meso and micro levels than ever before. Under the cover of a neoliberal, market and management-oriented word game, project planning and process control are practised vigorously. Social work offers a clear illustration of this development.' (Kunneman 1996, p.107, translation WB).

Kunneman states that the ideological focus shifted from solidarity to autonomy and self-management. This did not happen without consequences on professionalism in institutions. 'Professionals in the social sector are expected to be technically competent with effective practice methods to ensure the agreed output is achieved, the financier/customer is satisfied, and the subsidy continued' (p.107, translation WB).

Many employees in health care and social work, and also in education, will recognize this pressure on them. This may be unpleasant or even painful, because a dominating technical concept of professional work undermines essential qualities of the work. Kunneman refers to the phenomenon of 'illegal supervision': when workers with limited working time provide help and services in their own personal time. The complement of this phenomenon is constituted by 'workers who are not even willing or allowed to begin service provision if the initial assessment or intake shows that the client's issue will require a disproportionate amount of time, resources, and attention' (pp.107–108, translation WB).

It is clear that the functioning of social institutions is at risk. This is due to the application of business principles in public and nonprofit institutions, increased power of managers, and in many respects, a disproportionate balance of powers required for the well-being of organizations and workers.

When a business approach becomes predominant in an organization, strong influence of managers on professional workers negatively affects working conditions, service provision, and output. This is referred to as *managerialism*. (To those unfamiliar with this word, I suggest typing it into a search engine on the internet. I did so in January 2012, and a total of 894,000 hits were reported by the Google search engine!)

Taco Brandsen (1998) defines managerialism as

> a form of management…focused on economically defined efficiency and effectiveness and outcome-directed control…combined with ample power for managers to shift standards. This structure enables the manager to limit the powers of other professionals and to centralize control and authority within the organization. (pp.5–6, translation WB)

Brandsen considers managerialism as a form of neo-Taylorism (Taylor invented the conveyor belt for the Ford company): central regulation of work processes of a mechanical character, in which the manager thinks and the employees follow. This leads in the view of Kunneman (1996) to *a technical* concept of professionalism that jeopardizes content and significance of the social professions.

Kunneman pleads for revitalization and re-introduction of normative concepts in social professions. He emphasizes that the concept of *normative professionalism* was developed as a critical counterpart of technical concepts of professionalism.

> The critical character of the concept is based on the principle that, if anything, professionalism in social work implies a normative position, politically as well as existentially. This brings with it an appeal to make this position explicit, to justify it in a reflective way, and to use it as a measure for individual professional functioning. (Kunneman 1996, p.107, translation WB)

Brandsen and Kunneman gave early warnings about the destructive effects of managerialism, as also did Baart (2000), whose evaluation of 15 years of neoliberal social policy is discussed in Section 6.3.3.

In 2003, the warnings of Brandsen, Kunneman, and Baart were finally heeded because of the increasing complaints by professional workers, their clients, and their patients. Van den Brink (2003) gave voice to the dissatisfaction in a popular social magazine:

> Citizens and professionals are weighed down by the way in which institutions and organizations have operated since the 1980s. Today, many institutions work with a commercial, client-centred approach, marketing their 'products' (the services provided). The industrial model has been transplanted into the public sector. (van den Brink 2003, translation WB)

Van den Brink then referred to current problems:

> A top-down structure has been established, in which managers determine what the professionals have to do. When confronted with a problem, managers often come up with a so-called solution, but these solutions are often inappropriate or ineffective because the managers do not have the knowledge or experience in how to deal with such problems.

The solution is clear: 'Professionals should be given the room to work using their own skills, experience, and judgement, as well as involving the ordinary citizen whenever appropriate (van den Brink 2003, p.7, translation WB).

Today, social policy as the remedy for the expensive, uncontrollable Welfare State has lost its effectiveness. At first, this remedy worked well, but it now seems to be worse than the presenting disease or problem. In my opinion, neoliberal policy stimulated and strengthened actual processes of individualization, isolation, and selfishness in society, at the expense of collective awareness, solidarity, and equality – the three normative pillars under the Welfare State.

6.3.2 Growing critics and international movement

In 2007, social workers, social work teachers and social work researchers in Austria and in the United Kingdom joined together in a protest against the negative effects of neoliberal policy for social work and its clients in their countries. They also gained support from colleagues in other countries for their critical statements in the 'Vienna Declaration' and the 'Manifesto for a new engaged practice'.

These movements and their statements deserve a place in this book because of their social meaning and significance for the profession, as well as because of the clear description and examples they provide regarding the effects of neoliberal social policy on social work and its clients. Together with the Dutch example in Section 6.3.1, they provide material for a critical analysis of social work and its future.

In the 'Vienna Declaration' of Bakic, Diebäcker, and Hammer (2007), a clear stand is taken against economization and privatization of social work, as well as the undermining of social rights and solidarity of the citizens.

> The economization of social work is guided by the maxims of privatization and business-orientation. It is marked by a retrenchment of state support, the reduction or non-adjustment of social budgets, as well as growing constraints on social work orientations by economic and security logics. (Bakic *et al.* 2007, p.1)

These tendencies lead to an emphasis on consumption and market value, rather than recognizing the importance of the role that social context plays. 'Pressure for self-determination, self-responsibility and flexibility increase, while individual rights and systems of collective solidarity are [undermined, WB]' (p.1).

The Vienna Declaration contains six key challenges for social work:

1. *Loss of professional self-determination because of economic principles.* 'The pressure of cost-effectiveness and competitiveness seems to imply that increases in the efficiency of social work are indispensable. In any case, social work has to prove its utility in economic terms which, given the primacy of the economic, leads to the subordination of professional standards to business goals and the loss of professional self-determination of social work. *What is needed*: Priority for substantive and professional standards as opposed to economic rationales' (Bakic *et al.* 2007, p.2).

2. *Loss of quality of services because of standardization and a limitation on measurement.* This is the result of 'increasing bureaucratization, formalization and standardization of social work processes and activities in order to generate…data that comply with financing rules and secure the legitimization of social work. *What is needed*: An assessment of social work based on a qualitative frame of reference' (Bakic *et al.* 2007, p.2).

3. *Exclusion of clients because of a lack of resources.* 'Political decisions resulted in a lack of resources for social work and, subsequently, limitations of support [available in terms of] material, staffing and finances' (Bakic *et al.* 2007, p.3). This constrains professional work, and furthermore, changes its fundamental orientation and excludes certain people in need of help. *What is needed*: Social work resources available to all people facing difficulties or crises.

4. *Deficits in specialization within social work because of competition and efficiency pressures.* Cost-saving motives and competition pressures lead to a retreat to basic core competencies and a redefining of specialization. 'This is the parallel tendency to a deficit-oriented and stigmatizing construction of target groups that stands in the way of a critical-emancipatory concept of social work professionalism *What is needed*: Protection of a critical-emancipatory and general conception of social work professionalism through cooperation and exchange' (Bakic *et al.* 2007, p.3)

5. *Loss of professional options in the wake of the current dominance of administrative procedures.* 'Social work is subsequently shifted towards an emphasis on control, and furthermore, under the primacy of efficiency, is in danger of vanishing into bureaucratic administration. The one-sided emphasis on aspects of control and discipline results in a considerable weakening of professional options in social work. *What is needed*: Reflexive professionalism to protect from a one-sided instrumentalization' (Bakic *et al.* 2007, p.4).

6. *Loss of public critique and debate in the face of social work's depoliticization.* 'Internal discussions and political debate [regarding] social problems face strict time and economic limits…aggravated by intra-organizational hierarchies and the centralization of strategic tasks.' *What is needed*: Conditions and resources for public engagement with social problems (Bakic *et al.* 2007, p.4).

In July 2007, four colleagues (Jones, Ferguson, Lavalette, and Penketh) from three British universities (Liverpool, Stirling, and Manchester) published a manifesto entitled: 'Social work and social justice: a manifesto for a new engaged practice.'

The Manifesto begins with the statement that it is time to stop talking about 'the crisis of social work' and, instead, find more effective ways to move toward a more engaged practice.

> Social work in Britain today has lost direction. This is not new. Many have talked about social work being in crisis for over 30 years now. The starting point for this Manifesto, however, is that the 'crisis of social work' can no longer be tolerated. We need to find more effective ways of resisting the dominant trends within social work and map ways forward for a new engaged practice. (Jones *et al.* 2007, p. 1)

Many British social workers 'entered social work out of a commitment to social justice or, at the very least, to bring about positive change in people's lives. Yet increasingly the scope for doing so is being curtailed' (Jones *et al.* 2007, p.1)

In clear, direct formulations, the Manifesto describes the problems in British social work. The problems do not seem to differ much from those in Austria and the Netherlands. The work of social workers:

is shaped by managerialism, by the fragmentation of services, by financial restrictions and lack of resources, by increased bureaucracy and work-loads, by the domination of care-management approaches with their associated performance indicators and by the increased use of the private sector. (Jones *et al.* 2007, p.1)

The consequences of these are felt daily.

While these trends have long been present in state social work, they now dominate the day-to-day work of front line social workers and shape the welfare services that are offered to clients. The effect has been to increase the distance between managers and front line workers on the one hand, and between workers and service users on the other. (Jones *et al.* 2007, p.1)

The managers are heavily criticized: 'The main concern of too many social work managers today is the control of budgets rather than the welfare of service users, while worker–client relationships are increasingly characterized by control and supervision rather than care' (Jones *et al.* 2007, p.1)

According to the Manifesto, social work is at a crossroads. Choices for the future have to be made.

Down one road is managerialism and increased marketization, and with it, frustration and despondency for frontline workers…down the other [road] there is a possibility – and it is no more than that – for a renewed and regenerated social work that engages with the resources of hope available in the new collective movements for an alternative, and better world. (Jones *et al.* 2007, p.3)

Social work can learn from the emerging user movements and self-help groups.

In the last two decades, the growth of users' movements (like the disability movement and the mental health users' movement) has brought innovation and insight to our ways of seeing social and individual problems. These movements have developed many relevant and interesting approaches to dealing with service users' needs – collective advocacy, for example, or (in the mental health field) the Hearing Voices groups or user-led approaches such as the Clubhouse model. The fact that these models have come, not from professional social work but from service users themselves, emphasises that social work needs to engage with, and learn from these movements in ways that will allow partnerships to form and new knowledge bases and curricula to develop. (Jones *et al.* 2007, p.2)

The authors and subscribers of the Manifesto also search their own conscience.

The enduring crisis of social work in Britain has taught us many things. It has brought us to a state of affairs that nobody in their right mind could possibly view as acceptable. It has taught us that there can be no return to a past of professional arrogance and that progressive change must involve users and all front line workers. (Jones *et al.* 2077, p.3)

The Manifesto reminds us that 30 years of neoliberal policy have caused much damage and pain. A lot of repairing and healing has to be done.

As agents of change, senior managers have had their day. It has reminded us that budget dominated welfare systems are cruel and destructive of human well-being. The casualties are everywhere in the social work system amongst clients and users and social workers. (Jones *et al.* 2007, p.3)

The British workers learned a hard lesson that is also of value for their colleages elsewhere in the world.

These years of turmoil have highlighted that social work has to be defined not by its function for the state but by its value base. Above all it has been a stark lesson in the need for collective organization, both to defend a vision of social work based on social justice and also to defend the working conditions that make that possible. (Jones *et al.* 2007, p.3)

6.3.3 Pros, cons, and damage

Andries Baart evaluated in 2000 the effects of 15 years of neoliberal social policy on health care and social care in the Netherlands. He listed the most important changes, and demonstrated their pros and cons (Baart 2000). Although the evaluation dates from 2000, it is in my opinion still current for the situation today.

The 'six paradoxical developments' of neoliberal social policy are as shown in Figure 6.2.

6 paradoxal developments		
	+	**–**
1 More differentiation	precision, professionality, justification	fragmentation, passing on, bureaucracy
2 More methods & procedures	technical competence, predictability	depoliticization, intrumentalization
3 Bureaucratic fairness	equal treatment	distance, formalism, indifference
4 Market mechanisms & industrial thinking	standardization efficiency, payment	production, treatability, purchasing power
5 Instrumental calculations	planning & review	less narrativity, meaning, and "slow questions"
6 Status of the profession	professionalization status, respect	isolation, arrogance, distance

Figure 6.2 Six paradoxal developments in care and welfare in the Netherlands after 1985 (based on Baart 2000)

Details of the effects included in this overview are as follows:

1. *More differentiation.* There is more precision, professionalism, and specialization. There is also greater emphasis on accountability for one's work. However, there is increasing fragmentation and a loss of coherence. Accountability leads to bureaucracy. Management does not understand daily work experiences and tasks.

2. *More methods and procedures.* There is increased instrumental-technical competence, and a high grade of predictability. Negative effects are depoliticization of problems, standardization, and suppressed normative discussions.

3. *Bureaucratic fairness.* Treatment is more equal across similar cases. However, this results in greater emotional distance, indifferent treatment, and formality.

4. *Market mechanisms and industrial thinking.* Increased economic efficiency and cost control in upscaled institutions. Highly educated professionals are downgraded to the level of factory workers. Difficult cases with low chance of success are passed on to someone else or avoided altogether.

5. *Instrumental calculations.* Tight, managerial ropes bind practical work. Positive results are ease in planning and greater convenience. The downside is less room for narratives (people's stories), moral significance, and clients with so-called 'slow questions of life'. Problems are redefined into manageable institutional terms (see also point 2).

6. *Status of the profession.* According to Baart, professional groups in education, care, and welfare gained more status and respect in society, despite internal downgrading of the work. However, this was at the expense of face-to-face contact with ordinary people. Such contact is looked down upon.

Baart did not include education in his research, but as an experienced senior lecturer in higher professional education, I recognize many of these same effects in my field.

In my opinion the most negative effects of neoliberal social policy, however, are the disproportionate increases in power of managers and bureaucratic officials in institutions, the dominance of economic efficiency and control, and the resulting limiting effect on the action space of professional workers and the quality of services offered.

Twenty years of privatization and market mechanisms in Western countries with welfare states resulted in a new class of institutional managers. The managers surrounded themselves with a new bureaucracy of bookkeepers, public relations officers, system managers, and process controllers. They limited the action space of professional workers and saddled them with too many administrative duties. The managers' behaviour became a motivator for public and political expression of wishes in the Netherlands, such as more 'blue' on the streets (police), more 'white' at the beds (nurses), more contact hours in schools, and more helping hands in care homes for the elderly.

Because too many managers began using their power to line their own pockets, the Dutch parliament set a 'Balkenende Standard' for managers of public and nonprofit institutions. 'Balkenende' is the family name of the former Prime Minister, and the standard is his salary (approx. 200,000 euro per year), set as a maximum for managers of public and nonprofit institutions in the Netherlands. Today, it seems necessary for the parliament to make laws and enforce the standard, because moral appeal to managers and internal 'codes of conduct' have not been effective. In the meantime, many citizens, mostly those who are vulnerable or marginalized, pay a price for this abuse, and for the laborious functioning of vital social services and institutions. In such instances, people become isolated, forgotten, and left to their fate, while even the providing of elementary services in family care, elderly care, and care for the disabled (such as washing oneself, toileting, walking outside) is limited, as day care and youth care are hampered by a lack of screening of staff, supervision, and safety precautions.

Drawing 4 Social worker at a crossroads (© Henny Feijer)

6.4 Democratic and professional ways out and forward

Today, there are professional, public, and political discussions happening regarding neoliberal policy with its 'discipline of the market' and the consequences for professional functioning and quality of service provision. At stake is the viability and continuation of meaningful professional practices in and from workable and accessible public and social institutions. Section 6.4.1 offers a practical solution.

Social work has survived the era of neoliberal social policy until now, but does not come through completely unscathed. In social work, health care, and education, the balance between management and executive levels has been upset. The content of professional work and practice conditions need to be improved and protected in the coming years. In section 6.4.2 I discuss the current state of affairs of social work, and share my opinion on the matter.

6.4.1 A democratic way out

The way in which health care, social work, and educational institutions are managed needs to be changed and improved in order to prevent further professional and social damage. It is possible to organize and manage work processes in a more intelligent, humane, and reflective way than can be observed today in many social, educational, and medical institutions. This can and must be done efficiently, and by careful spending of public money.

Evelien Tonkens (2008) provides a way out of the stranglehold of neoliberal policy for social institutions, professional workers, and their customers. Although Tonkens' analysis and recommendations are based on the situation in the Netherlands, they also can be relevant for other countries in comparable situations.

According to Tonkens, four structural problems have to be solved in order for professional workers in public and social institutions to have the freedom they need to do their work in an effective and efficient manner. These structural problems are:

1. Increasing costs of the public sector in comparison with the market sector.

2. The 'immaturity' of democracy.

3. Ambivalent duties for professionals.

4. Destructive ways of organizing institutions.

Relevant to *cost*, it is inevitable that labour productivity in the market sector grows faster than in the public and social service sectors. This is a result of different characteristics of these sectors. For example, because of technological advances, 'assembling a computer can be done in less and less time; teaching and washing people cannot' (Tonkens 2008, p.1, translation WB). To rectify this, professionals have to work faster and put in more hours. To ensure this is done, control and supervision are increased and intensified. This results in less efficiency, because the professionals have to waste time dealing with bureaucratic red tape. Meanwhile, workers are pulled between achieving and accounting, rather than being given the room and appreciation they need to do their jobs well.

The *immaturity of democracy* refers to democratic inability in everyday life. Many people cannot cope with criticism or differences of opinion. Citizens who speak their minds, institutions [that] refuse to accept criticism, and lack of debate are all signs of an undeveloped, immature democracy.'

Professional workers are saddled with *ambivalent duties*.

> They are expected to empathize, but not get too personal... At the same time, we expect helping professionals to intervene in the life of others. If he does not intervene successfully and someone is harmed or dies, the worker is blamed. (Tonkens 2008, p.2, translation WB)

Many social institutions are *organized in a destructive way* because of expensive and de-motivating bureaucratic mistrust.

> Indication is disconnected from performance. Performance is specialized and fragmented into multiple tasks and functions... On the one hand it is enriching, but on the other hand, too many people are confronted with the fact they do not fit the mold. (Tonkens 2008, p.2, translation WB)

The result is: Citizens are confronted with too much administration and rarely make actual contact with people. They often feel unknown, and their problems are not recognized or understood.

> Professionals spend a lot of time consulting, reporting, and coordinating, and do not have the opportunity to oversee the whole process. Protocol, rules, and regulations put workers in straitjackets. The paperwork is given priority because workers need to protect themselves from possible lawsuits. (Tonkens 2008, p.2, translation WB)

Tonkens (2008) concludes with the following recommendations, with which I fully agree:

1. Acknowledge the fact that public and social services are labour intensive, and therefore costly.

2. Institutions, workers, and managers should welcome, organize and learn from comments and criticism. 'An effective democracy cherishes criticism, dissent, and controversy, from the consulting room to the newspaper' (Tonkens 2008, p.3, translation WB). Disagreement and resistance should not be considered taboo. Rather, people's opinions deserve respect, attention, and a response. Citizens and professionals should be heard when policy changes occur.

3. 'When professionals are given a broad task, allow them to use their own discretion' (Tonkens 2008, p.3, translation WB) and give them room to work according to their own professional judgement.

4. 'Organizational proliferation has to be tempered with a simple adage: everything is based on personal contact and the relationship between professionals and citizens (students, patients, clients, residents). All the work should serve this directly. If it does not, it should be abolished. Passionate care needs to return to service provision, and the soul is needed back in the classroom' (Tonkens 2008, p.3, translation WB).

The realization of these recommendations is vital to the conditions under which professional social work will be conducted in the years to come.

6.4.2 Moving forward as a profession

The social work profession has paid a price for being an instrument of neoliberal policy for more than 30 years. Researchers such as Wallace and Pease (2011), Carey (2009), Baart (2000), Aronson and Smith (2011), and Harris (2008) have attempted to estimate the damage to social work, hoping that 'through this research, a more sophisticated understanding of the impact of neoliberalism on social work will contribute to the revitalization of critical social work' (Wallace and Pease 2011, p.1). As demonstrated in Section 6.3.2, social workers are uniting and organizing themselves to try to limit the damage to the profession, and to re-socialize the institution of social work.

The theorists among the workers provide their contribution by debating the future of social work. In 2010, the International Online Journal *Social Work & Society* dedicated an issue to the elimination of the 'social' in social work from the mid-1970s, with a selection of international papers.

In the introductory article, Roose, Coussée, and Bradt (2010, p.2) argue that the relation between individual life worlds and collective life has changed drastically during the last decades, with consequences for the position of social work:

> People are incited to take more individual responsibility and an instrumental attitude towards social integration. In this instrumental approach, the professional expertise of social work does not include broader social questions, but mainly focuses on the question 'how should we adapt to these changes?' But which kind of citizenship does social work propagate then? The instrumental approach might offer a methodical certainty and a clearly defined professional knowledge base, but it can also induce frustration, uncertainty and feelings of powerlessness. The 'social' in social work tends to erode and disappear (Lorenz 2005) and is regarded as a consequence of a correct (evidence-based) solution to individual problems. As a consequence, we witness an increasing dualism between those who have a way with individual competition and those who cannot cope due to a lack of resources (time, money, capacities).

According to Roose *et al.* (2010), emphasizing the social dimension in social work can bring social workers to an ambivalent and uncertain position balancing rights and obligations, interests of clients, objectives of labour market partners and those of agencies. However,

> social workers (and their clients) are not powerless. For social work interventions are not only answers to social problems, but are closely connected to defining and constructing these problems. As a consequence social work interventions themselves help to create the individual and societal horizon of legitimate aspirations (Mahon 2002) and define the bounds of what is possible. (Roose *et al.* 2010, p.3)

In many countries, social work is a public–private cooperation and an ensemble of different organizations and institutions. 'This gives the opportunity to create a broad social forum for discussion and disagreement, to raise counter-arguments ... and to break open the boundaries of social work and the often introspective social work debates' (Roose *et al.* 2010, p.3). The special issue of *Social Work & Society* makes it clear that the debate can go in different directions.

Hans van Ewijk (2010) offers an interesting contemporary approach. He argues that social work, in its role of 'supporter'

> should position itself in the centre of the post-modern quest: the social-psychological disorientation, the lack of meaning, and the problems of isolation and exclusion. Modern professionalism is not about demarcating and regulating, but much more about "Entgrenzung" and openness'. (van Ewijk 2010, p.22)

van Ewijk refers to the current complex state of society (he calls it 'State of Complexity') that creates new social and socio-psychological problems for a fast-growing number of people:

> So far, mental health and punitive approaches are the dominant answers, bringing back the complexity to reductive strategies. A local social support structure as a mix of informal support, volunteers and social workers seems to be a reasonable, cost effective alternative, accepting complexity as the starting point and trying to support people to cope with this complexity and to survive in a highly socially sensitive society. (van Ewijk 2010, p.28)

The social worker is needed as a supporter, coach, and activator of networks, systems, and individuals. In this context the social worker 'is a broad profiled expert, combining the classic traditions of social professions: social pedagogy, social work and using resources from [various] philosophies of life' (p.28).

van Ewijk's approach is appealing because it refers to contemporary developments in wealthy countries. However, because of this it is a limited approach, not applicable in poor countries. Although I understand his preference for embedding social work in local social support structures, in my opinion it is not wise to promote this unconditionally in wealthy countries as long as their social infrastructure is ruled by efficiency-dominated neoliberal social policy.

I would also like to refer to Gerard Donkers' Integrative Theory of Changing (see Section 3.4.5) in which the core task of social workers is to empower people, organizations, and communities by (creating conditions for) strengthening their self-regulating abilities. Because Donkers formulates duties and tasks of social work one (abstract) step higher than van Ewijk, his vision is more independent of current (political) developments. In my opinion, this is the appropriate level at which to formulate ways for social work to continue supporting human rights, equality, and democratic principles for all people worldwide.

During its 9th annual conference in Czech Republic, the International Social Work & Society Summer Academy (TiSSA) (see www.tissa.net) discussed the matter of 'Politics of Identity: The Changing Face of Social Work'.

Hans-Uwe Otto, leading theorist of social work and founder of TiSSA, is of the opinion that

> social work's future identity depends on its ability to achieve political acceptance for its reflexive self-definition corresponding to quality requirements and standing up to prevailing social challenges. For this purpose, a yardstick needs to be found for a critical analysis of social work both in relation to its functions and to its practical stance against the reproduction of social inequality. In particular, the problem of finding a normative basis needs to be addressed as a precondition for designing an action framework for problem-oriented interventions. (Otto 2011, p.1)

As usual, Otto plays both sides of the card: this theme

> concerns problems of professionalization and organization on the one hand, and political empowerment of service users on the other hand. This relates to the question of how a model of critical social work can be substantiated and how practice can confront the growing tendencies in market-oriented social policies, defining self-responsibility as a task for service users as individuals. (Otto 2011, p.1)

This is not without social consequences:

> In all countries one can observe an increase in the number of people affected by poverty and unemployment with particularly devastating consequences for children and young people. Against this background, the question has to be answered which model of identity social work can develop to assert itself against structures dominated by criteria of efficiency, effectiveness and very often driven by managerial power positions. (Otto 2001, p.1)

Otto formulates relevant, contemporary key questions of societal political nature. They are key questions for social work and social policy. It is obvious that they could not, and were not answered during one conference of only one group of scientists, lecturers and social workers. These questions are part of the on-going debate within the international social work community.

6.4.3 Think global, act local, and behave social!

Driven by technological, economic, social, and political forces, the process of globalization spreads across the world and changes the relationships between persons, groups, organizations, institutions, companies, national states, and international bodies. Many effects, especially the negative ones, are felt in everyday life at a local level, and in the consulting rooms of helping professionals.

While the slogans of Freedom, Change, Democracy, and Justice are being proclaimed once again, this time on the streets and squares in North Africa and the Middle East, a growing number of people in Western countries desire to get rid of neoliberal policy and the 'scourge of the market' as the managing principle in the public and social sector because of its destructive effects on social and democratic values and standards which Arab societies are demonstrating for.

These cries for freedom, democracy, and solidarity occur as nuclear plants in Japan melt down, as oilfields continue to burn in heavily exploited, polluted, and neglected communities in Africa and Asia, as so-called 'Western diseases' and AIDS claim many victims, and as tsunamis, earthquakes, hurricanes, and Icelandic volcanic ash clouds threaten civilization as we know it.

Taken together, all these events appear to be a huge worldwide confrontation encompassing all aspects of human life: natural, physical, social, economic, technological, and ideological. Undoubtedly, this massive global confrontation will have a significant impact on the course of the globalization process.

Social work is caught in the middle of these developments, which makes the profession extremely challenging and demanding. Additionally, social work is vulnerable as a profession because of its dependency on public, scientific, and political support.

It is a continuous challenge to uphold the initial ideals of social work: to support persons, groups, organizations, and communities, to stimulate participation, empowerment, and democracy, and to contribute to a fair and humane society. To continue doing these things, it is vital to think 'big' (i.e. international), to act 'small' (in one's own community), and to be a living example of a good person and citizen yourself.

For these reasons, my final words are: *Think global, act local, and behave social!*

References

Aronson, J. and Smith, K. (2011) 'Identity work and critical social service management: balancing on a tightrope.' *The British Journal of Social Work 41*, 3, 432–448.

Baart, A. (2000) 'Zich afstemmen op de onafgestemden – Hoe professionals marginalen kunnen bereiken.' ['Adjust to the Unadjusted – How professionals can reach people in a marginal position.'] *Sociale Interventie 2000*, 1, 4–21.

Bakic, J., Diebäcker, M. and Hammer, E. (2007) 'Vienna Declaration on economisation and professionalism in social work.' *SW&S News Magazine 2007*, July. Available at www.sozialearbeit.at/archiv.php?documents=true, accessed 25 January 2012.

Bennis, W., Benne, K., Chin, R. and Corey, K. (1969, 1974, 1985) *The Planning of Change*. New York: Holt, Rinehart and Winston.

Blachman, M. (2004) 'John T. Pardeck (ed.): Family health social work practice: A macro level approach' (Review). *Journal of Sociology & Social Welfare 31*, 1, 217. Available at http://findarticles.com/p/articles/mi_m0CYZ/is_1_31/ai_n6065946/, accessed on 25 January 2012.

Brandsen, T. (1998) 'De manager als moderne held.' ['The manager as a modern hero.'] *Tijdschrift voor de Sociale Sector 9*, 52, 4–7.

Brink, G. van den (2003) 'Oplossingen komen niet meer uit Den Haag.' ['Solutions do not come anymore from "The Hague."'] Interview. *Zorg + Welzijn 3*. Available at www.zorgwelzijn.nl/web/Actueel/Nieuws.htm?contentid=13045, accessed on 24 January 2012.

Bronfenbrenner, U. (1979) *The Ecology of Human Development: Experiments by Nature and Design*. Cambridge, MA: Harvard University Press.

Bronfenbrenner, U. (1994) '5 Ecological models of human development.' *International Encyclopaedia of Education, Vol. 3*, 2nd edition, pp.1643–1647. New York: Elsevier.

Bruin, E. de (2005) 'Wat wil de mens?' ['What does man want?'] *NRC Handelsblad, Wetenschap en Onderwijs 2005*. Available at http://wjsn.home.xs4all.nl/tekst/steven-reiss.htm, accessed on 20 January 2012.

Cambridge Dictionaries Online (2011) Available at www.dictionary.cambridge.org, accessed on 8 September 2011.

Carey, M. (2009) 'The quasi-market revolution in the head – ideology, discourse, care management.' *Journal of Social Work 5*, 4, 341–362.

Center for Developmental Science (2012) Available at http://cds.unc.edu/mission.htm, accessed on 19 January 2012.

Cozijnsen, A. and Vrakking, W. (2003) *Handboek verandermanagement – Theorieën en strategieën voor organisatieverandering.* [*Handbook change management – Theories and strategies for organizational change.*] Deventer: Kluwer.

Donkers, G. (2005) *Veranderkundige modellen.* [*Models of Change.*] 11th edition. Baarn: H. Nelissen.

Donkers, G. (2010) *Grondslagen van veranderen – Naar een methodiek zonder keurslijf.* [*Foundations of Changing – Toward a methodology without straitjacket.*] Den Haag: Boom Lemma uitgevers.

Donkers, G. (2011) *Organisatieontwikkeling als proces van zelfregulering.* [*Organization Development as a Process of Self-regulation.*] Nijmegen: Stichting De Parel.

European Foundation on Social Quality (1997) *Amsterdam Declaration on the Social Quality of Europe.* Available at www.socialquality.org/site/html/declaration.html, accessed on 22 January 2012.

European Foundation on Social Quality (2012) *Introduction to the theory of Social Quality.* Available at www.socialquality.org/site/html/theory.html , accessed on 22 January 2012.

Ewijk, H. van (2010) 'Positioning Social Work in a Socially Sensitive Society.' *Social Work & Society 8*, 1, p.22–31.

Gent, B. van (1991) *Basisboek Andragologie.* [*Basic book Andragology.*] Meppel: Uitgeverij Boom.

Gevel, A. van de and Goor, H. van de (1989) *Bestuur & Systeem – Een inleiding in de bestuurskunde.* [*Government & System – An Introduction to Public Administration.*] Leiden: Stenfert Kroeze.

Gray, M. and Webb, S. (eds) (2009) *Social Work, Theories and Methods.* London: Sage Publications.

Gray, M. and Webb, S. (eds) (2010) *International Social Work, Four-Volume Set.* London: Sage Publications.

Habermas, J. (1981) *The Theory of Communicative Action, Volume 1.* Cambridge: Polity Press.

Harris, J. (2003) *The Social Work Business.* London and New York: Routledge.

Harris, J. (2008) 'State Social Work: Constructing the Present from Moments in the Past.' *British Journal of Social Work 38*, 4, 662–679. Available at http://bjsw.oxfordjournals. org/content/38/4/662.abstrac, accessed on 22 January 2012.

Healy, L. and Hall, N. (2007) 'International Organizations in Social Work.' In L. Wagner and R. Lutz (eds) *Internationale Perspektiven Sozialer Arbeit.* Frankfurt and London: Iko-Verlag für Interkulturelle Kommunikation IKO.

Herrmann, P. and Maesen, L. van der (2008) *Social Quality and Precarity: Approaching New Patterns of Societal (Dis-)Integration.* Working Paper No. 1. The Hague and Amsterdam: European Foundation on Social Quality.

Houston, S. (2009) 'Jürgen Habermas.' In M. Gray and S. Webb (eds) *Social Work, Theories and Methods,* pp.13–22. London: Sage Publications.

Hortulanus, R. (1997) 'Lokaal sociaal beleid in Nederland.' ['Local social policy in the Netherlands.] *Sociale Interventie, 2*, 66–84.

IFSW (1994) *The Ethics of Social Work Principles and Standards.* Adopted by the IFSW General Meeting in Colombo, Sri Lanka, 6–8 July 1994. Available at www.ifsw.org, accessed on 8 September 2011.

IFSW (2000) *Definition of Social Work.* Adopted by the IFSW General Meeting in Montreal, Canada, July 2000. Available at www.ifsw.org/p38000208.html, accessed on 15 January 2012.

IFSW and IASSW (2004a) *Ethics in Social Work, Statement of Principles.* Approved at the General Meetings of IFSW and IASSW in Adelaide, Australia. Available at www. ifsw.org/f38000324.html, pdf file (4 pages) accessed on 15 January 2012.

IFSW and IASSW (2004b) *Global Standards for the Education and Training of the Social Work Profession.* Adopted at the General Assemblies of IASSW and IFSW, Adelaide, Australia. Available at www.ifsw.org/p38000868.html, pdf file (24 pages), accessed on 15 January 2012.

Jones, C., Ferguson, I., Lavalette, M. and Penketh, L. (2007) 'Social work and social justice: a manifesto for a new engaged practice.' *SW&S News Magazine.* p. 1–3.

Kamp, M. van der (1993) 'Methodiekontwikkeling: concepten en trajecten.' ['Development of methodology: concepts and routes.'] In M. van der Kamp *et al.* (eds) *Methodiekontwikkeling: concepten en trajecten,* pp.7–16. Utrecht: Uitgeverij SWP.

Kunneman, H. (1996) 'Normatieve professionaliteit: een appèl.' ['Normative professionalism: an appeal.'] *Sociale Interventie* 3, 107–112.

Laan, G. van der (1993) 'Methodiekontwikkeling: over systematiek en doelgerichtheid.' ['Methodology development: systematics and purposiveness.'] In M. van der Kamp *et al.* (eds) *Methodiekontwikkeling: concepten en trajecten,* pp.33–51. Utrecht: Uitgeverij SWP.

Leeuwen-den Dekker, P. van and Centre for Social Adaptation for Homeless Women in Kiev (2006) *The Eight Steps Model in Practice.* Utrecht: Netherlands Institute of Care and Welfare. Available at www.movisie.nl //Publicaties//NIZW/691/8stepsmodel. pdf , accessed on 24 January 2012.

Lewin, K. (1951) *Field Theory and Social Research.* New York: Harper & Brothers.

Lippitt, R., Watson, J. and Westley, B. (1958) *The Dynamics of Planned Change. A Comparative Study of Principles and Techniques.* New York: Harcourt, Brace and Company.

Lorenz, W. (2005) 'Social work and a new social order: Challenging neo-liberalism's erosion of solidarity.' *Social Work & Society 3,* 1, 93–101.

Maesen, L. van der and Walker, A. (2005) 'Indicators of social quality: Outcomes of the european scientific network.' *European Journal of Social Quality 5,* 1/2, 8–24.

Magnusson, D. (2000) 'The Individual as the Organizing Principle in Psychological Inquiry: A Holistic Approach.' In Bergman, L., Cairns, R., Nilsson, L.-G. and Nystedt, L. *Developmental Science and the Holistic Approach,* Chapter 3 (pp.33–48). Mahwah, NJ: Lawrence Erlbaum Associates.

Mahon, R. (2002) 'What Kind of "Social Europe"? The Example of Child Care.' *Social Politics 9,* 4, 342–379. Cited in Roose, R., Coussée, F. and Bradt, L. (2010).

Maslow, A. (1943) 'A Theory of Human Motivation.' *Psychological Review 50,* 370–396.

Maslow, A. (1987) *Motivation and Personality,* 3rd edition. New York: Addison-Wesley. (Original work published 1954.)

Maslow, A. and Lowery, R. (eds) (1998) *Toward a Psychology of Being,* 3rd edition. New York: Wiley & Sons. (Original work published 1990.)

Mizrahi, T. and Davids, L. (eds) (2008) *Encyclopaedia of Social Work,* 20th edition. National Association of Social Workers and Oxford University Press. Also available in a digital version.

Murphy, J. (1994) 'A Postmodern Justification for Holism in Social Work Practice.' In R. Meinert, J. Pardeck and W. Sullivan (eds) *Issues in Social Work: A Critical Analysis,* Chapter 4. Westport, CT: Auburn House.

Nelissen, N. and Wit, H. de (eds) (1991) *Het verkennen van sociale problemen.* [*Exploring Social Problems.*] Vierde druk. Zeist: Kerckebosch BV.

Nieuwenhuis, M. (2010) *The Art of Management Deel 2* [part 2], 10th edition. Uitgever Marcel Nieuwenhuis. ISBN 978-90-806665-2-8. See also www.the-art.nl, accessed on 8 September 2011.

Nieuwenhuis (2012) Available at http://123management.nl/0/040 _mensen/a400_ mensen_20_motivatie_modern.html, accessed on 16 January 2012.

NIZW Beroepsontwikkeling (2006) *Klaar voor de toekomst, een nieuwe beroepsstructuur voor de branches welzijn & maatschappelijke dienstverlening, gehandicaptenzorg, jeugdzorg, kinderopvang.* [*Ready for the Future, a New Professional Structure for Social Work and Social Services.*] Utrecht: NIZW.

Otto, H. (2011) *Politics of Identity – The Changing Face of Social Work.* Available at www. tissa.net/tissa2011/t11_plenum.htm accessed on 8 September 2011.

Parton, N. and O'Byrne P. (2000) *Constructive Social Work: Towards a New Practice.* New York: Palgrave Macmillan.

Penna, S., Paylor, I. and Washington, J. (2000) 'Globalization, Social Exclusion and the Possibilities for Global Social Work and Welfare.' *European Journal of Social Work 3,* 2, 109–122.

Pincus, A. and Minahan, A. (1973) *Social Work Practice: Model and Method.* Itasca, IL: F.E. Peacock Publishers Inc.

Prochaska, J. and DiClemente, C. (1982) 'Transtheoretical therapy: Toward a more integrative model of change.' *Psychotherapy: Theory, Research & Practice 19,* 3, 276–288.

Ramsay, R. (1999) 'Toward a common paradigmatic home: Social work in the 21st century.' *Indian Journal of Social Work 60,* 1, 69–86. (Special Issue: 'Social Work in the Next Millennium.')

Reiss, S. (2000) *Who Am I? 16 Basic Desires That Motivate Our Actions and Define Our Personalities.* New York: Berkley Books (Penguin USA).

Roose, R., Coussée, F. and Bradt, L. (2010) 'Going beyond the bounds of possibility: Questioning the delimitation of the social in social work.' *Social Work & Society 8,* 1., p.1–5.

Skehill, C. (2008) 'Editorial.' *British Journal of Social Work 38,* 4, 619–624.

Staatsblad [State Bulletin of Acts, Orders and Decrees] (2010) *Social Support Act.* Changed by Act of 30 November 2006 (Stb1. 644), 10 April 2008 (Stb.164), 2 April 2009 (Stb. 229), 25 June 2009 (Stb. 346), and 4 June 2010 (Stb. 269).

Step4ward, Institute for the Reiss Profile (2011). See under 'Our main activities'. Available at www.reiss-profile.co.uk, accessed on 24 January 2012.

Tonkens, E. (2008) 'Bevrijd vaklui uit de bureaucratie.' '[Liberate professionals from the bureaucracy.'] *De Volkskrant*. Available at www.zorggeenmarkt.nl/ opinie/080913tonkens-volkskrant-bevrijd-vaklui-uit-bureaucratie.pdf/, accessed on 22 January 2012.

Tweede Kamer der Staten Generaal (Dutch Parliament) (1999) *Welzijnsnota 1999–2002 - Kamerstuk 26477 nr.2*. Available at https://zoek.officielebekendmakingen.nl/kst-26477-2.html, accessed on 22 January 2012.

Wallace, J. and Pease, B. (2011) 'Neoliberalism and Australian Social Work: Accommodation or Resistance?' *Journal of Social Work 11*, 2, 132–142. Available at http://jsw.sagepub.com/content/11/2/132, accessed on 20 January 2012.

Warren, M. (2006) 'Globalisation, exploitation, and the local church.' *Australian eJournal of Theology 7*. Available at http://aejt.com.au/_data/assets/pdf_file/0009/395136/ AEJT_7.13_Warren_Globalisation.pdf, accessed 15 January 2012.

Wikipedia (2011) Available at http://en.wikipedia.org/wiki/Emic_and_etic, http:// en.wikipedia.org/wiki/Columbia_University_School_of_Social_Work, and http://en.wikipedia.org/wiki/Globalization, accessed on 8 September 2011.

Wikipedia (2012) Available at http://en/wikipedia.org/wiki/social_work_knowledge_ building, accessed on 15 January 2012.

Zaltman, G. and Duncan, R. (1977) *Strategies for Planned Change*. New York: Wiley.

Zwart, C. and Middel, B. (2005) *Omvormen van jezelf en de wereld om je heen – Een uitnodiging tot de ontwikkelkunde*. [*Transforming Yourself and the World Around You – An Invitation to the Developmental Theory*.] Assen: Van Gorcum.

Subject Index

Author Index